Lerner and Loewe's
My Fair Lady

"An Englishman's way of speaking absolutely classifies him, The moment he talks he makes some other Englishman despise him."
– Henry Higgins

George Bernard Shaw famously refused to permit any play of his "to be degraded into an operetta or set to any music except its own." Allowing his beloved *Pygmalion* to be supplanted by a comic opera was therefore unthinkable; yet Lerner and Loewe transformed it into, *My Fair Lady* (1956), a musical that was to delight audiences and critics alike. By famously reversing Shaw's original ending, the show even dared to establish a cunningly romantic ending.

Keith Garebian delves into the libretto for a fresh take, and explores biographies of the show's principal artists to discover how their roles intersected with real life. Rex Harrison was an alpha male on stage and off, Julie Andrews struggled against her popular image as a chaste diva, and the direction of Moss Hart, a sexually ambiguous dazzler, contributed to the musical's sexual coding.

Keith Garebian is a freelance literary and theatre critic, and an award-winning author and poet.

The Fourth Wall

The Fourth Wall series is a growing collection of short books on famous plays. Its compact format perfectly suits the kind of fresh, engaging criticism that brings a play to life.

Each book in this series selects one play or musical as its subject and approaches it from an original angle, seeking to shed light on an old favourite or break new ground on a modern classic. These lively, digestible books are a must for anyone looking for new ideas on the major works of modern theatre.

Also available in this series:

Coming soon:

For Nonnie Griffin and David Roche

Lerner and Loewe's
My Fair Lady

Keith Garebian

Routledge
Taylor & Francis Group

LONDON AND NEW YORK

First published 2016
by Routledge
2 Park Square, Milton Park, Abingdon, Oxon OX14 4RN

and by Routledge
711 Third Avenue, New York, NY 10017

Routledge is an imprint of the Taylor & Francis Group, an informa business

© 2016 Keith Garebian

British Library Cataloguing-in-Publication Data
A catalogue record for this book is available from
the British Library

Library of Congress Cataloguing-in-Publication Data
A catalog record for this title has been requested

ISBN: 9781138960060 (pbk)
ISBN: 9781315660448 (ebk)

Typeset in Bembo
by Out of House Publishing

Contents

Preface

This book takes a new look at *My Fair Lady* as a romantic musical comedy. It assumes that readers already know the literary source of the musical – George Bernard Shaw's didactic play *Pygmalion*, which received its English-language premiere in 1914, a year after the play had debuted in German in Vienna and Berlin. This book also presupposes that readers are familiar with the back-story about George Bernard Shaw's staunch refusal (after Oscar Straus's 1908 musical adaptation of *Arms and the Man* as *Der tapfere Soldat*, or *The Chocolate Soldier*) to permit any other play of his "to be degraded into an operetta or set to any music except its own" (McHugh 2012: 4). Rather than being a detailed production history, my book takes a fresh look at the libretto, the two stars' interpretations, and the biographies of Rex Harrison, Julie Andrews, and their director Moss Hart in order to delve deeper into certain aspects of the musical. I argue that it is Higgins rather than Eliza who is visually and aurally dominant, though it is Eliza whose singing voice tears through the strong tissue of male homo-sociality in the libretto. And it is Higgins who regains his dominance at the end (after bouts of uncertainty and disillusionment), though this dominance may, in fact, be illusory, as it becomes clear near the end that gruff Higgins overcomes obstacles in his own nature to realize that he has fallen in love in his peculiarly non-sexual way. Moreover, Eliza allows him to think he is dominant while she craftily submits to him in the way Shakespeare's Katherine submits at the end of *The Taming of the Shrew* to Petruchio. The Lerner-and-Loewe ending thereby becomes more cunningly romantic than first thought, and even if this could reasonably have caused Shaw to blanch or blush, this musical resolution creates its own justification as it manufactures its own fable.

Often overlooked in the discussion of this musical are the intersections of biography and role in the cases of the two leading players and the director. Rex Harrison's life history was in some ways a version of Eliza's ascent from low class to a higher one, as well as an internalized version of Higgins's. Julie Andrews, in turn, also rose above her family's proletarian social station in England, gaining caste, as it were, by becoming a Broadway star. And, more intriguingly, her biography bears startling intersections with the fictional life of Eliza Doolittle, though where Eliza's mother is clearly absent from Shaw's fable, Andrews's mother (despite frequent physical absences from her home and children) was a strong artistic influence. Many studies of this musical fail to consider the contribution of its director, Moss Hart, to the re-coding of the fable. Like his two stars, he was born to English parents and rose from humble beginnings to extraordinary levels of fame and fortune, exemplifying wit, urbanity, and grace. He made great contributions to the American musical (*Lady in the Dark*), and his screenplay of *A Star is Born* (for George Cukor) is considered one of the greatest ever written for an

American film. His memoir, *Act One*, remains one of the finest of its type, and, of course, his artistic reputation reached its acme with *My Fair Lady*. But not all was golden in his life: in spite of his numerous awards for stage and screen, he suffered from manic depression and struggled with issues of sexual identity in private. So, my book charts new territory for these three icons and for the legend of *My Fair Lady*.

Acknowledgments

I thank David Roche in Toronto for his supportive friendship, his witty knowledge of musical theatre, and his most useful comments and advice during early and later versions of my manuscript. Working with Taylor & Francis has been a congenial experience. Ben Piggott was encouraging from the minute he saw my first draft, and he continued to impart very useful and smart editorial advice so that I could trim my manuscript without losing its central focus. Robert Whitelock was my excellent copy-editor, while Zeba Talkhani, Stacey Carter, and Kate Edwards oversaw the production process for Routledge, causing me no pain yet much gain.

Rex Harrison

Alpha male

It is a fact universally acknowledged that the greatest Henry Higgins in the history of *My Fair Lady* was Rex Harrison. It is also a fact almost universally acknowledged that Harrison, in real life, was as chauvinistic, domineering, sneering, patronizing, and narcissistic as Higgins on stage. As he himself noted in a memoir, almost all his major roles were "of the self-centred type, who, in Higgins's words, 'desires nothing more / than just the ordinary chance / to live exactly as he likes / and do precisely what he wants'" (Lerner 1956: 56). In other words, his major roles were usually cads, though he strove to get an audience "to find something sympathetic in them, so they can identify, and even grow to *like* them" (Harrison 1991: 211). In his case, the actor's medium was certainly himself – and what a self that was! England made him but he, in turn, remade himself, becoming, like Henry Higgins, an artist, husband, and father who demanded that he be in unchallenged control of things. Born the youngest in a family of three (he had two sisters) on March 5, 1908 ("the final flamboyant years of the Edwardian era") in Huyton, a little village outside Liverpool, Reginald Carey Harrison was conditioned to a life of genteel poverty rather than of ostentatious wealth. Family folklore had it that his mother's family "was descended from the great actor Edmund Kean (1787–1833), who was, in turn, descended from the poet-composer Henry Carey." And though Harrison brushes this claim off as "a bit of family nonsense, if you ask me, and remains an unsubstantiated rumour" (Harrison 1991: 2), he was fond of claiming that his antecedents were virtually aristocratic. He told Patrick Garland (who directed a revival of *My Fair Lady* in London and for a tour in 1980–1) that his grandfather owned a great Georgian house called Belle Vale Hall, which a very young Harrison used to visit, enjoying the croquet lawns, lakes, tennis court, and rookery. Harrison's grandparents had been used to provincial style before the family fortune foundered. Harrison's father William was forced to declare bankruptcy, and it was rumoured that Belle Vale was turned into a jam factory and finally demolished to make way for a housing estate. This Dickensian image of genteel poverty may have been the most accurate one. In any event, Rex was brought up in a semi-detached house, and attended a little kindergarten and then a private school before making it into Liverpool College. However, the family myth about ancestral wealth was carefully cultivated by his sister Sylvia, Countess de la Warr; if this myth cannot be definitively proved or disproved, the fact remains that the family reflected "an affluence and indifference to the realities of life which had been passed down through recent generations" (Garland 1998: 67).

The counter-myth – that Harrison's father was a butcher – also lacked credible evidence. William Harrison was a tall, straight-backed man who habitually wore a cornflower (the Harrow school flower) in the buttonhole of his Norfolk jacket. As his famous son wrote: "He had played hockey for

England and run the hundred yards in 10.5 seconds, and had studied engineering in Germany, but throughout his life he did very little work – I think because there was nothing he really wanted to do" (Harrison 1975: 15). William (like Rex, born third but in a larger family) possessed charm, drifting through life "with a singular nonchalance, a certain arrogance, combined with an indifference to work" (Garland 1998: 67), and it seems that some of these character or personality traits were inherited by his son. What transcends both myths is the incontrovertible fact that Rex Harrison's early years "were transformed and romanticized" (Garland 1998: 67). After a bout of childhood measles, he lost most of the sight in his right eye, so he was not sent to Harrow (where his father had been) but was kept at home and sent to a local school. Naturally, being so much at home and being the youngest, he became something of a mother's boy, and he often wondered later whether that was how he first grew accustomed to having women around in his life – "in direct contradiction" to the line in the famous song from *My Fair Lady*: "You Should NEVER Let a Woman in Your Life!" (Harrison 1991: 4).

Early in boyhood, he decided that he was not a Reggie or a Reginald, and asked his mother if she would be so kind as to address him as Rex in future. In his memoir he explains that "this regal choice" was neither influenced by the heroic deeds of an ancient king nor even by admiration of George V, the reigning king of England at that time. Nor was it taken from a cinema or place of entertainment called the Rex. Instead it was but "a childish, arbitrary choice, which may, at best, have occurred because I heard someone calling his dog to heel" (Harrison 1991: 2). At seven, he wished his father (whose war job entailed making armour plate for battleships) wore "a glamorous uniform, festooned with decorations for heroic deeds performed 'at the front'" (Harrison 1975: 17). Little wonder, then, that Rex fell in love with Uncle Vivian, who wore a rough khaki uniform with puttees, was an excellent sniper for the Canadian forces, and was full of stories of "unbelievable dangers, to say nothing of whisky and lice." There was a large age-gap between Rex and his two sisters (Sylvia was four years older than he, and Marjorie eight), so from as early as age 8 or 9, Rex presented solo productions at home after seeing pantomime at the Hippodrome in Liverpool. But his first performance was startlingly original in its utter confidence: it consisted of no performance at all, except for repeated bows to the adulation and applause of his family. Star billing, it seems, came naturally and precociously to Rex Harrison, making him a legend in his own juvenescent mind.

As a stage-and-screen star, he was an actor who revelled in certain roles, especially sophisticated ones as an upper-class gent. The image of Harrison as the very model of an English gentleman was wholeheartedly accepted by Hollywood in the late 1940s, but Harrison was not necessarily comfortable living out the iconic role at all times. Garland reports that when Harrison's fifth wife, Elizabeth Rees-Williams, showed him round the beautiful mansion in St. Jean-Cap Ferrat, he suddenly exclaimed: "I can't possibly live here, Elizabeth, I'm only an actor" (Garland 1998: 62). A renowned Hollywood film agent once related a magical evening spent with Harrison, the actor's sixth wife (Mercia Tinker), and a group of friends at a luxurious French restaurant, where for most of the evening Harrison talked passionately and lucidly about the glories of Proust's *A la recherche du temps perdu*, though there was no concrete evidence that he had read Proust in the original. On another occasion, the same agent witnessed Harrison working through an entire wine list in very stylish dumb show with a waiter who spoke only French and who assumed that Harrison was speaking French as well (Garland 1998: 63). Such displays of style and authority were part and parcel of Rex Harrison, who was able to parlay them to perfection as Henry Higgins, the incomparable epitome of English arrogance – even though Higgins's flamboyance was more linguistic than sartorial, meant to dominate and intimidate rather than to edify or humanize.

Acting filled Harrison's career at Liverpool College, where his first role was as Flute, the bellows-mender, who doubles as Thisbe in *A Midsummer Night's Dream*. For one who was notoriously uneasy about any insinuation about homosexuality, this cross-dressing part of Thisbe (played in a rather large blond wig, an ample bosom, long dress, and with a lisp) seems like an ironic biographical footnote, but it does set off its own intriguing suggestions. In his first autobiography, *Rex*, the actor writes of falling in love "with the small boy playing Titania, only because he looked so beautifully like a girl" and of following him everywhere backstage (Harrison 1975: 20). But what might first seem like latent homosexuality was really something else – displaced or misaimed theatrical illusion – for Harrison's affection "did not go beyond the costume, and when he took it off I had no time for him at all. Nor can I remember anybody following me about as Thisbe!" (20). The last sentence smacks of self-defensiveness that is, perhaps, symptomatic of a phobia that became more pronounced later in life, but Harrison at the time of the Thisbe experience was already a teenager, and so any discomfort with sexual ambivalence or ambiguity would not have been uncommon for a youth his age.

Harrison's progress as a professional actor followed the common trajectory of English actors: parts in repertory (the

Liverpool Repertory in his case), touring productions of plays that had been hits, and then larger parts in London, where a career can be made or broken. Drawing-room sophistication became his cachet in such comedies as S. N. Behrman's *No Time for Comedy* (1939) and Noel Coward's *Design for Living* the same year. Although Harrison had outstanding Broadway and Hollywood successes, he did not ascend the brightest heaven of artistic invention till *My Fair Lady* in 1956. This was not his first foray into the world of George Bernard Shaw: that distinction came with his performance as Cusins in Gabriel Pascal's black-and-white film version of *Major Barbara* (1941), an artistic failure. Leslie Howard would precede him as Higgins on film in *Pygmalion* (1938), co-directed by Anthony Asquith and Howard. The film's camera-work and montage effects now seem dated and strange, with quick dissolves and fades, but its great achievement is its literary sophistication (derived, of course, from Shaw), just as its most startling innovation is the un-Shavian ending, where the highly dramatic conflict between Higgins and Eliza is rendered in a manner that runs contrary to Shaw. Heavy script-editing and romantic acting by Howard shift the register of Higgins, and though he is superficially the proud, devilish chauvinist who returns at the end to imperiousness, Howard gives him an achingly soft vulnerability and a slower delivery to add weight to his words.

Both these touches are far outside Rex Harrison's interpretation even at its best, but the probable cause is really the difference in the actors' temperaments and techniques. As a film actor, Howard was all about English romanticism, often with reserve, and sometimes with grace notes of frailty or vulnerability. Rex Harrison could also be romantic on film, and he always cut a graceful figure, but his acting was not notable for suggestions of human frailty or aching vulnerability. He had vibrant power, suave sophistication, and in his best genre – which was really high comedy – he was (as Richard Burton claimed) "the highest of high comedians," one in whom the acting and off-stage personality were inextricably bound together (Burton 2012: 636). Both men exemplified what Camille Paglia calls "the well-bred English 'gentleman,' a word that cannot be perfectly translated into any other language" – but which was illustrated by the likes of Cary Grant, David Niven, and Michael Wilding, for instance (Paglia 1991: 533). Both Howard and Harrison had a singular male beauty, were witty and polished, and typified a kind of heterosexual glamour. And both had qualities of what Paglia calls "smoothness and elongation" in terms of manner, appearance, and ectomorphic height. Howard was not averse to showing a feminine softness – as he did in *Romeo and Juliet* (1936), *Intermezzo* (1939), and *Gone with the Wind* (1939) – but this type of anti-machismo was beyond Harrison's range or crafted stage-and-screen personality. Harrison was more suited to play kings or popes, aristocrats rather than plebeians, emperors rather than common men, although he remained forever English no matter whether he was pretending to be King Mongkut (*Anna and the King of Siam*, 1946), Julius Caesar (*Cleopatra*, 1963), or Pope Julius II (*The Agony and the Ecstasy*, 1965). Leslie Howard also remained English in his characterizations, but he was able to subdue his masculinity when required, which is something Harrison could not match. In *Staircase*, the 1969 film adaptation of Charles Dyer's two-hander about an aging gay couple who own a barber shop in London, Harrison and Richard Burton (who was playing his partner) camp it up like a sideshow attraction. Although Harrison insists in a memoir that he and Burton would do their "damnedest to play homosexuals without in any way being 'camp'" (Harrison 1991: 201), Burton contended that his co-star kept becoming less queer daily until he was "hardly queer at all – he's almost professor Higgins" (Burton 2012: 234). But Burton is as guilty as Harrison in parodying mincing homosexual behavior. As a result, both actors are in embarrassing bad taste, as neither ever really wants to submit to his role or play for essential truth. Their parody becomes an affront to gay sensibility, but the actors (particularly Harrison) appear intent on stressing that they are so straight that even pretence at homosexuality would be self-violation.

My Fair Lady would allow Harrison to remain in control of his image as an alpha male, though it must have come as a shock to him to discover later that he was not the first choice for Higgins. He was certainly *among* the first to be considered for the role. Stanley Holloway claims in his memoir *Wiv a Little Bit o'Luck* (1967) that Noel Coward was given top consideration, followed by Michael Redgrave (Holloway 1967: 68). In fact, Redgrave, who could sing, agreed to play the role but then balked at a two-year commitment on Broadway. The only person involved with *My Fair Lady* who had wanted Harrison was Gabriel Pascal, but he was now dead. Harrison was not a singer, "nor was he an altogether sympathetic choice for a large general audience" (Bach 2001: 344). His Hollywood film career had come to a standstill in 1948 because of various scandals: while married to Lilli Palmer, he was having an affair with American actress Carole Landis, who killed herself with an overdose of barbiturates – some believed because of unhappiness caused by Harrison. Gossip columnists turned against him, and "sexy Rexy" (as he was dubbed) became *persona non grata* in the Hollywood film community. Harrison got the role "only after every other actor in England had been asked to play it, starting with Noel Coward and ending with John Gielgud" (Bach

2001: 345). Coward's biographer Sheridan Morley says that it was Coward himself who suggested Harrison to the producers (Morley 1974: 343). Lerner had promulgated a white lie in his autobiography by claiming that the actor had always been everybody's first and only choice. Lerner "was writing when Harrison was still alive, still playing the part in revival, and still one of the most difficult actors anyone – including Moss [Hart] – had ever encountered" (Bach 2001: 344).[1]

To begin with, he was not easy to recruit for the role. When Alan Jay Lerner and Frederick Loewe visited the actor backstage in London where Harrison was performing in a long run of *Bell, Book and Candle* (1954) opposite Lilli Palmer (his wife at the time), they felt "an unmistakable strain and *froideur* in the air, and discovered that the two stars were unofficially separated off-stage because Harrison was in love with the brilliant comedienne Kay Kendall, whom he joined every night after he and Palmer had completed their curtain calls." It was not easy to persuade him to undertake a leading musical role, especially one as important as that of Henry Higgins. Harrison let it be known promptly that he hated the two songs already completed for the show ("Please Don't Marry Me" and "Lady Liza"), and the two composers, to their credit, agreed that the songs "were slick and

---

1 Rex Harrison was not the first choice for the film version. Producer Jack Warner had wanted Cary Grant for Higgins and Audrey Hepburn for Eliza, and offered Grant $1.5 million dollars to play Higgins. Grant turned this offer down, telling Warner: "No matter how good I am, I'll either be compared with Rex Harrison, and I don't think I'll be better than he is, or I'll be told I'm imitating him, which isn't good for him, or for me. And not only will I not do it, but if you don't hire Rex, I won't even go and see it" (Eliot 2004: 342).

instead of being acting pieces set to music, they were skin deep and clever word games" and were by no means final products. (Lerner 1978: 58). Next, they had to convince him that Leslie Howard had not been the definitive Higgins, with Lerner arguing that Howard's Higgins wrongly indicated a full awareness of Eliza's pain and of "the strange stirrings within himself." Harrison finally agreed that Howard had been a touch too romantic and sympathetic, writing several decades later: "Alan said he didn't believe that Higgins had the slightest idea what was worrying Eliza, and I agreed with him. I had to convey the genuine amazement of the man when he discovers that the girl has any feelings of any kind at all" (Harrison 1991: 122).

The next question was whether Harrison could sing well enough for a Broadway musical. Though the actor had appeared in musicals in London in the early 1930s and had even sung in them, his minimal singing ability had been forgotten. At the invitation of Lerner and Loewe, he attempted a verse of "Molly Malone" to piano accompaniment, to the composers' quick approval. Lerner noted a "tenor timbre, which meant it would carry over an orchestra," and he and Loewe later discovered that Harrison's sense of rhythm was faultless. In short, Harrison was "instinctively musical" (Lerner 1978: 59), but his dithering left the composers hanging around London for weeks, though they were able to use this time to visit Covent Garden and learn how cockney rhyming slang works – which was especially useful for Eliza's number "Wouldn't It Be Loverly?" with its clever dialect touches. The cockney habit of inserting words into the middle of other words also became a source of inspiration for new coinings, though he changed "absobloodylutely" into "absobloomin'lutely" in the lyric for "Wouldn't It Be Loverly?"

On the Sunday of their fifth week in London, they received a call from Harrison, who suggested that they all go for a wintry stroll in Hyde Park, where Lerner and Loewe had to jog to keep up with him for almost three hours. Harrison kept "chattering away," while Lerner and Loewe were "panting away." Then all at once, the actor stopped, turned to them, and declared: "All right. I'll do it." Lerner and Loewe were too exhausted to show their joy (Lerner 1978: 63).

In mid-February, Lerner and Loewe left London with "the Shaw rights in one hand, commitments from Rex Harrison, Stanley Holloway, and Cecil Beaton in the other, two less songs than [they] had arrived with and a year's work ahead of [them]." Though they may not have anticipated it, they also had Rex Harrison's alpha-male temperament ahead. A preliminary contract was drawn up by Herman Levin at Claridge's Hotel on March 18, guaranteeing Harrison a salary of $3,000 a week, plus 10 percent of the gross box office receipts between $30,000 and $50,000. He was also guaranteed a minimum of six weeks' employment, or $18,000 if the show had to close early. He would receive first-star billing, though whoever was selected for Eliza could be co-starred if Levin chose. The contract was to run a year (McHugh 2012: 28).

The terms favored Harrison, of course, and when Stanley Holloway (for Alfred Doolittle) insisted on equal star billing with Harrison, the latter was completely unwilling to allow it because he felt that Holloway's name didn't mean anything to Broadway audiences and that the role of Doolittle should automatically get feature billing (McHugh 2012: 32). Consequently, there was no warm collegiality between the two actors, and Holloway even took his sour feelings to the press. In his second autobiography, Harrison makes no mention of the row about star billing and claims, instead, that

Holloway was miffed because Moss Hart seemed to ignore him in order to devote most of his attention to Julie Andrews, who was struggling with her role (Harrison 1991: 129–30).

Holloway and Harrison were perfect foils to each other on stage, and offstage they were direct contrasts as well. Harrison was playing a Shavian version of aspects of himself, whereas Holloway was playing a determinedly extrovert dustman. Both roles in the musical are, in a sense, alpha males, but Doolittle (in the words of Holloway) was a low-class "great, glib yapper when it comes to righting the world's wrongs. To him an argument is an enjoyable challenge so long as he can out-talk the other fellow" (Holloway 1967: 45). In contrast, Holloway himself was radically different from the alpha male he was playing on stage. Unlike the dustman, Holloway loved working, preferred discussion to argument, drank moderately, and loved being married and having a pleasant, affectionate home. Holloway identified with Doolittle only in performance, whereas Harrison identified with Higgins even offstage on many an occasion.

The two men hardly ever met in the theatre after rehearsals were finished, and met very little in the play itself. Apart from the scene where Doolittle "sells" Eliza to Higgins for his experiment, and another small scene, they never came across each other in the play and "usually met only at the final curtain." Socially, they golfed together occasionally and went along to a few parties, but they "certainly did not hobnob" because of the difference in their ages and their social tastes (Holloway 1967: 90).

There was a much greater or merely a natural affinity between Harrison and Lerner, because both were high-strung men "dedicated to serial matrimony," according to Moss Hart's biographer Steven Bach, who pointed out that

Lerner would have eight wives and Harrison six. "Together we've supported more women than Playtex," Lerner is said to have once quipped. Each man "thought himself – divorces and suicides notwithstanding – a compassionate expert in the care and handling of the female, not unlike the egocentric and oblivious Higgins" (Bach 2001: 347). Harrison was "as likely to address a wife – anybody's wife – with 'You bitch!' as with any other endearment, which seemed part of Harrison's 'unique approach to human relations'." In *A Damned Serious Business*, Harrison admits generously to enjoying the experience of having been a mama's boy in his boyhood very much, though he isn't certain about the reasons for liking and marrying women (what he terms "this 'little weakness'"), suggesting first that it was because of his very attractive mother's influence, before offering two other possible motives: "Perhaps it is simply that I like their companionship. I like their understanding. I like them because you don't have to explain everything to them. They know. They're intuitive – and realistic." But Harrison immediately modifies his generosity: "I don't think it would be fair to say that I've been dependent on the women in my life – they've looked after me, and I've looked after them. Damn well, too!" (Harrison 1991: 4). Harrison was the very incarnation of male chauvinism, so much so that Higgins's "A Hymn to Him" (written by a man who already had six wives by then and sung by a man who was to have six of his own wives eventually) seemed to be a partial version of Rex Harrison's autobiography.

2

Julie Andrews

Chaste vocal diva

With Harrison's signing a contract on March 10, 1955, the only missing elements were a leading lady and a director. Herman Levin claimed that while in London, he and his collaborators had auditioned "maybe fifty girls, including a nobody named Petula Clark." All were rejected and the search resumed in New York (Bach 2001: 347). It was known at the time that Harrison had approval of his leading lady and of his director. Harrison agreed to Herman Levin's insistence in London that he pre-approve directors in order to expedite things, so the names of John van Druten, Alfred Lunt, Robert "Bobby" Lewis, Peter Glenville, Tyrone Guthrie, Cedric Hardwicke, Cyril Ritchard, and Hume Cronyn received Harrison's approval for serious consideration. Moss Hart's name was floated offhandedly, to which Harrison reacted: "Oh, Moss Hart. He wouldn't be much good, would he?" Like most actors who rewrite history to cover up their egotistical manias and follies, he lavished praise on Hart in his autobiography, writing that he "was an extraordinarily talented man, and immensely respected, and we were very lucky to have him on the show" (Harrison 1991: 125). The unvarnished truth was that he gave tepid pre-approval to Hart as "a fallback in the unlikely event no one else worked out" (Bach 2001: 347).

The list dwindled quickly. Van Druten was not terribly excited by the idea of the musical, though he added he might be later – without clarifying what he meant. Ritchard was too busy with work at the Met. "Others were unavailable, found the project ill-advised, or were, like Lunt and Guthrie, not entirely right for a musical, or for Lerner and Loewe" (Bach 2001: 347–8). This left Moss Hart who, alas, had been recently ill and was rumoured to be collaborating with Harold Rome on a musical of his own. While facing this problem, Levin, Lerner, and Loewe turned to casting the female lead. The two biggest female musical comedy actresses of the time were Ethel Merman and Mary Martin, but it was clear that Merman's assertive personality and belting voice were ill suited to Eliza. Martin had been Lerner's actual choice two years earlier, in 1952, and he actively pursued her, confiding to Pascal in a letter that, "although there are undoubtedly others who can play it, I do feel that anybody after Mary is second choice" (McHugh 2012: 9). Eliza was one of the greatest parts in a musical, and Martin was one of the greatest musical performers. It seemed like "a perfect marriage" to Lerner, who added: "It doesn't bother me at all that she is American because if the King's English as taught to her by the Prof doesn't seem completely compatible with her, neither was it with Liza in the play. And the cockney she can do easily." He was so enthusiastic about her that he declared: "I'm ready to do anything short of homicide to see Mary as Liza" (McHugh 2012: 9–10). In case Martin turned the role down, the alternatives were Judy Garland, Deanna Durbin, and Dolores Gray. A meeting with Martin; her husband, Richard Halliday; and their guest, couturier Mainbocher, was arranged in New York at the apartment of Lerner's mother. Martin was still appearing on Broadway in *Peter Pan*, so it was shortly before midnight when the invited trio walked in and listened to the five songs completed for the musical: "The Ascot Gavotte," "Just You Wait," "Please Don't Marry Me," "Lady Liza," and "Say a Prayer for Me Tonight." As it transpired, Martin was disenchanted with the songs she heard, privately lamenting to her husband, "Richard, those dear boys have *lost their talent*" (Bach 2001: 343), and that put an end to her interest in the show.

No one was quite sure who first suggested Julie Andrews for Eliza, but all three men took credit for the casting. Credit was also paid in some quarters to Cy Feuer, producer of *The Boy Friend* (Andrews's first stage musical hit). Years later, even Andrews was confused about where the credit should go (Bach 2001: 348), though there is no question that Rex Harrison should not get any share of that credit because, as Lerner describes in his memoir, Harrison made it "vociferously clear" numerous times in rehearsal that Andrews was well below his stature as a performer and did not really deserve to share the same stage he trod and dominated.

Julie Andrews's family background had some remarkable similarities with the impoverished, sordid backgrounds of Eliza and Alfred P. Doolittle. Named after her grandmothers Julia (Ward) and Elizabeth (Wells), Andrews was born on October 1, 1935 in the village of Walton-on-Thames in Surrey. Her legal surname was that of her stepfather, Ted Andrews, a large, heavy-drinking, violent Canadian who was the second husband of her mother, Barbara Ward Morris. However, Julie did not take kindly to "Pop," and continued to idolize Edward Charles (Ted) Wells, whom she thought was her real father until 1950, when her mother revealed that

Julie was the result of a one-time liaison with an unnamed family friend (Andrews 2008: 120–3). Barbara had two sons (Christopher Stuart and Donald Edward) by Ted Andrews, but she fell into frequent bouts of depression, feeling that she was deprived of a successful career as pianist and piano-teacher. Her own family history had been sordid. Although her father (Arthur Morris) was a popular poet and used his musical skills to entertain villagers at concerts, fund-raisers, and other functions, he was a physically abusive, drunken womanizer. Her mother (Julia Ward) suffered depression and deserted her family. So, this family picture is more working class or middle class than upper class, and very much in keeping with Shaw's image of an England where poverty or genteel poverty was a radical social and spiritual evil.

Julie Andrews does not dwell inordinately on this oppressive part of family history, electing, instead, to pay sentimental tribute to her Dad (Ted Wells) for exposing her and her younger brother John to the wonders of nature and to music. Ted had "a light, 'bathroom baritone' voice of which he was somewhat proud." He also whistled well and had a genuine interest in poetry. Although not really demonstrative of his love for his children, he never gave them reason to doubt it. Because he and Barbara did not get along, there was domestic tension, exacerbated by Barbara's periodic absences from home. When World War II broke out, Julie and her brother were in the care of her father and Aunt Joan while Barbara was often away performing concert parties with Ted Andrews, and it was not long before Barbara left her marriage for good, leaving young Julie to suffer from nightmares. Although her father remained close to her and her younger brother John ('Johnny'), usually spending half summer vacations with them, she didn't see him as much as she would have liked. "But what I got was quality time. He's responsible for the saner part of my nature. Everything that was real and good, *he* gave me," she said in an interview (White 1998: 110).

Before the Blitz began in earnest, Barbara sent for Julie to come to London to live with her and Ted Andrews, with young Johnny left in the custody of his father. London was "an awakening of some sort" – as if she had suddenly grown up. Her parents lived in a dark apartment, where the kitchen had a dusty window with bars, suggesting a cage. There was a bedroom and a small living room – and there was Ted Andrews, a man she deemed "a new shadow" in her life (Andrews 2008: 27). The black sheep of his family, he had endured an abused childhood. Of florid complexion, he was "compact, powerful," with "a sort of bullet head, and fast-receding sandy hair. For the theatre he wore a toupee, blending the hairline with color." Because of his volatility at the time, he was a startling contrast with her gentle dad (whose pet-name for her was "Chick") (Andrews 2008: 48). Julie was ill at ease with Andrews, meeting his "occasional overtures" with shyness or outright derision (Andrews 2008: 27). Her reactions did not obscure the fact that she was searching for concrete proof of love from her mother. Ted Andrews was incapable of offering that love. In fact, his alcoholism turned him into something of a monster on occasion because he twice attempted to get into bed with her, resulting in the girl's putting a lock on her door.

The one solace for her was her singing voice, which had phenomenal range and strength, especially for one so young as she was. A throat specialist ascertained that she had an almost adult larynx (Andrews 2008: 38). To his credit, Ted – who was a baritone himself – gave her singing lessons before sponsoring lessons for her at the Cone-Ripman School and then with his own voice teacher, Madame Lilian Stiles-Allen, in London. She laid a solid foundation for Julie's vocal development, teaching her breath control, shifts of gear, vocal placement, and holding the last note. Madame also paid a lot of attention to Julie's clarity of diction, making a point that singing was musical speech. "If you can't hear a singer's words, it is like a body moving without legs to carry it" (Stirling 2007: 22). The range, accuracy, and tone of the girl's voice amazed her. Julie possessed the rare gift of absolute pitch, and right up to the age of 14 had a four-octave range (22). For Madame, technique mattered most, and sometimes her rigorous coaching drove Julie to tears of frustration – perhaps a useful emotional memory that could be exploited in the role of Eliza when she is driven to the point of exhaustion and tears by Higgins's phonetic exercises.

Julie's professional career began when she was only 12, with a performance on BBC radio and a contract to sing the aria "I am Titania" from *Mignon* in a glamourous new musical revue, *Starlight Roof* (1947–8), at the London Hippodrome, with an all-star cast. On opening night, October 23, 1947, her mother bought her flowers for luck, and given her huge success that night ("Prodigy with Pigtails" and "Pocket-Money Star Stops the Show!"), violets took on a new meaning for her in the years that followed, culminating in Eliza Doolittle's violets. During the early part of the run, she did a ghastly screen test for the American producer Joe Pasternak, who had made all the Deanna Durbin films. But she was no Durbin; nor was she a Shirley Temple. However, Julie felt it more important to be wise and talented than to be pretty, and in 1948 she became the youngest solo performer ever to participate in a Royal Command Performance before the Queen. It was clear that her first Pygmalion, stepfather Ted, was by now overtaken by his young Galatea – a point borne out palpably when he later gave up show business altogether to become a traveling salesman.

Radio, music hall, pantomime, and concerts were useful training. Having played a princess in *Aladdin* (1951) and the title role in *Cinderella* (1953), she was already, in a sense, preparing to take on Eliza's magical transformation, though, of course, she did not know this at the time. After all, *My Fair Lady* incorporates the Cinderella fable in telling its story of a common flower girl groomed and educated to pass herself off as a duchess at the Embassy Ball. Julie's career seemed to have peaked with Cinderella, however. Her youthful "freak" voice kept changing; her formal education was virtually non-existent; and, trained to be decent and polite, she felt like a house pet: "inside there was a locked-up individual, doing all the moves and trotting out the form like a hamster on a wheel" (Andrews 2008: 155). But *The Boy Friend* came along at the right time. The Sandy Wilson musical was syrupy and romantic, but affectionate and affecting in telling the story of Polly Browne, the most popular student at Madame Dubonnet's finishing school on the French Riviera, who falls in love with a poor bellhop. As it turns out, he is really descended from aristocracy, so all turns out well in the end – rather like a fairy tale. Julie was not part of the London run, but after Anne Rogers (the London Polly) was unwilling to leave the London production for Broadway, Vida Hope (director of the show) made a point of seeing *Cinderella* at the Palladium and convinced Cy Feuer (American producer of *Guys and Dolls* and other hits) to consider Andrews, which he did, offering her a two-year contract to play the role of Polly Browne on Broadway. Only 18 at the time, she insisted on a one-year contract because she was afraid of feeling homesick, but Cy Feuer was impressed by her singing and perfect pitch: "There was no piano lead-in, no instrument to guide her to the right note, but she hit the note dead center every time. The music followed her." That was amazing in itself, but "even more impressive was her voice. She had a glorious soprano voice that filled the theater. On top of that she was cute" (Feuer 2003: 193).

Before she and her fellow cast-members of *The Boy Friend* left for New York, Sandy Wilson took her and her real-life boyfriend at the time to dinner. He was struck by her perfect poise and control far ahead of her years, and later wrote that as he watched and listened to her, she struck him as being "someone as remarkable in her way as Gertrude Lawrence." He realized that she would be a star on her own: "It was nothing that she said or did, and she certainly betrayed no symptoms of egotism or ambition; she simply had about her an unmistakable air of cool, clear-cut determination" (Stirling 2007: 55–6). It was clear to him that it was going to be the top or nothing for her, and that she knew exactly where she was going. Wilson was probably magnifying and embroidering his impressions because, though Andrews certainly had pluck, poise, and vocal charisma, she was not yet self-assured about stage acting, and she certainly had no idea at the time that she would soon be heading for the top of musical theatre in America.

She debuted on Broadway in the Sandy Wilson musical on September 30, 1954, taking at once to her director, Vida Hope ("a loving den mother") and the show's English contingent. Cy Feuer was concerned that the show, which had been a big hit in London, lacked the punch required for Broadway. Andrews was struggling with her role as Polly, and, inexperienced at "breaking down" a script, she resorted to trying to emulate the other women and indulging in semaphore acting. When Hope and Wilson were fired during rehearsals, Feuer took over like a drill sergeant, tightening the show till it was sharp and clean. Andrews's performance needed immediate attention because it was "floundering," with "disjointed moves that didn't come naturally." On the day of the opening (September 30, 1954), Feuer took her out on the fire escape of the theatre and demanded that she drop all her "nonsense with the hands and the eyes and the head." He urged her to be natural and believe everything she said on stage (Feuer 2003: 196). Andrews was smart enough to appreciate his contribution. Opening night, September 30, 1954, was the eve of her nineteenth birthday, and it was the night that marked her as a new star on Broadway's Milky Way. Each song won an ovation, and the brisk tempo and crisp, giddy fun of the show, far brisker than that of the more delicate one in London, provoked the audience to ecstasy – as did Andrews's performance. The standing ovation grew raucous, and people danced the Charleston down the aisles as they exited the theatre. Brooks Atkinson declared in the *New York Times* that it was she who gave the show "its special quality . . . She keeps the romance very sad. Her hesitating gestures and her wistful, shy mannerisms are very comic. But by golly, there is more than irony in her performance. There is something genuine in it, too." Writing in the *Herald Tribune*, Walter Kerr thought her perfect: "With a blonde Marcel, the largest amount of blue eye-shadow I have seen anywhere, and hands clasped winsomely just above her right knee, she breathes lunatic sincerity" (Stirling 2007: 64). Ten days after the opening, Julie Andrews glanced up at the marquee to read: "*The Boy Friend* – with Julie Andrews."

She learned significant things about performing during the run: "how to cement the humorous moments in the show, and the value of being real when playing comedy" (Andrews 2008: 180). As she neared the end of her one-year run, she was informed by Dick Lamar, a representative of Lerner and Loewe, that the team was working on a musical version of *Pygmalion* and would like her to meet with them. What she did not know then was that she was not the first choice for Eliza: with Mary Martin nixed as Eliza, the names of Deanna Durbin and Dolores Gray had been floated as possibilities (Holloway 1967: 97), but once Lerner, Loewe, and Herman Levin saw Andrews in *The Boy Friend*, they grew ecstatic. To Lerner, she was dazzling: "From the moment she set foot on the stage, one could see she fairly radiated with some indefinable substance that is the difference between talent and star." Her gifts of a charming and flexible soprano voice, immaculate diction, elegance in dance, and graceful move-ment were stylish and went "far beyond the dialogue, the role, or the play" (Lerner 1978: 52).

At her audition, she sang "Getting to Know You" and read some of the script in a cockney accent. Impressed by Lerner's charisma and exquisite manners (though he was often dif-ficult to fathom) and Loewe's Viennese charm, she was capti-vated by some of the songs for the show, especially "Just You Wait" and "Wouldn't It Be Loverly?" She did not know at that moment that she was about to undertake "one of the most difficult, most glorious, most complex adventures" of her life, or that she would be "guided through the daunting forest of self-discovery by several of the kindest, most brilliant giants one could ever hope to meet" (Andrews 2008: 182). If her words make her sound like sugary Maria von Trapp from *The Sound of Music* or like fairy-tale Cinderella charmed into a fantasy world, her gilded superlatives are understandable in context. Both Maria and Cinderella get their men, but Eliza

Doolittle was going to be quite a different sort of woman: a dominant vocal diva in terms of song, yet one subordinated most of the time to an alpha-male snob, while longing "for experience and for desire itself" – as Stacy Wolf perceptively notes about this character and the Guenevere that Andrews would later play opposite Richard Burton's Arthur in *Camelot* (Wolf 2002: 153).

3

Moss Hart

Sexually ambiguous dazzler

Moss Hart was considered for director only after Lerner and Loewe had completed "I'm an Ordinary Man." He was no ordinary man himself. Collaborator with George S. Kaufman on such hits as *Once in a Lifetime* (1930), *You Can't Take It with You* (1936), and *The Man who Came to Dinner* (1939), and the one who crafted *Lady in the Dark* (1941 – a musical well ahead of its time), Hart was already an extraordinary man of the theatre, even before he created his own romantic fable as "an upward-striving, rags to riches" outsider with "a whole catalog of Horatio Alger virtues and rewards" (Bach 2001: xi). Hart was an artful dramatist "whenever he took up his pen" and a "resourceful" entertainer who "rehearsed his dinner table bon mots while waiting for the guests to arrive" (Bach 2001: xii). He liked to joke: "I was born on Fifth Avenue – the wrong end!" Actually, he was born on October 24, 1904 in a New York tenement at 74 East 105th Street, a neighborhood of "dray wagons, pushcarts, and immigrants" (Bach 2001: 3–4). Hart branded his birthplace "shabby gentility," though evidence shows it was more a case of "bare subsistence."

His English-born maternal grandfather, Barnett (Barney) Solomon (originally Salamon, or Salaman), "had confounded immigrant cliché by working his way not up but down from comfortable respectability in England to near-penury in New York" (Bach 2001: 4). Given to occasional bouts of nostalgia for England, when not steeped in rage or depression, Barnett resorted to storytelling as an antidote to the "dispiriting realities of the Land of Liberty" (Bach 2001: 6). This resource evidently was passed on to his grandson Moss, along with Barney's enthusiasm for Charles Dickens and Shakespeare. Moss's faintly English accent, inherited from his forebears, sounded sissified and affected to his peers at school, and this peculiarity was heightened when "a certain theatrical lilt acquired from his Aunt Katie bumped up against the dropped aitches of his father's cockney, an accent whose usefulness lay almost entirely in the future of a girl not yet born named Julie Andrews" (Bach 2001: 11). Throughout his life, Moss Hart would have "an overpolished manner of speaking sabotaged by echoes of the Bronx in everyday words."

Hart would later admit to being not merely unhappy growing up, but "deeply disturbed." Poor at athletics, he learned to play the piano and ukulele, performing in parks and polishing his knack for storytelling. At 12, he won first prize in a school public speaking contest, and at 17, he set about becoming an impresario, though artistic and economic failure (particularly with *The Beloved Bandit* in 1925) made him feel like a "full-fledged failure at eighteen" (Hart 1959: 162) and a has-been at 21. However, he continued to look and act like a tall, slender dandy with a high forehead; bold nose; dark, wavy hair; expressively arched eyebrows; and a taste for flamboyant attire. "No stripe was too vivid, no plaid too vivacious" (Bach 2001: 32). All his friends and professional acquaintances found him to be an ideal companion, "a man of great warmth, a friend who could be relied on to provide help when needed, a witty – but not malicious or cynical – commentator on current events and all things theatrical" (Brown 2006: 81).

Hart enjoyed limited success as an actor (notably as a cheap cockney trader in a 1926 New York revival of Eugene O'Neill's *The Emperor Jones*, with the great actor Charles Gilpin in the lead role) but it was as a director and playwright (in collaboration with George S. Kaufman, "master of the destructive jest," as Brooks Atkinson noted [Bach 2001: 57] that he scored Broadway hits. Eventually awash with money, Hart moved his parents and brother Bernard to the opulent Waldorf Astoria Hotel, while he took "a nine-room tower apartment with multiple fireplaces and a semi-circular turret window that displayed the city below like an electric map in which all roads led to Times Square" (Bach 2001: 75–6). Having internalized his earlier hard times "as a private humiliation," he was now signaling how well the American Dream worked in making him a member of a superior social caste or class.

But newfound wealth and social prestige did not gild his private life, despite his increasing awards (including Academy Award nominations for writing *Broadway Melody of 1936* [1935] and *Gentleman's Agreement* [1947]). He suffered unpredictable and debilitating mood swings, leading to acute depression, and he continued to struggle with his ambiguous sexual identity. His public image bedazzled many, but privately he was a mass of neurotic problems. Success was itself a source of stress for him. He once remarked:

> The great mystery of unhappiness is not the story of a failure. A man who is a failure complains about fate, about bad breaks, and you can understand it. But when

you're completely successful and you're unhappy, it
becomes a mystery. Most of the successful people I know
are unhappy.

(Brown 2006: 187–8)

After he won the Pulitzer Prize for *You Can't Take It with You*,
he was depressed: "I practically had to be carried feet first
to my analyst's couch" (Brown 2006: 188). Was he more of
an actor than a man – akin to the classic dandy presented by
writers such as Baudelaire, Flaubert, Mallarmé, Swinburne,
Pater, Wilde, and Coward?

Like Oscar Wilde, he seemed to worship form in a social
life that often resembled theatre – as with his large mono-
grams, prodigal displays of furnishings, and extravagant shop-
ping expeditions. And, as with the dandies mentioned above,
he did not have an unequivocally defined romantic or sexual
identity. His interest in men exceeded his interest in women
until later in life. Even into his early forties, he would tell
women who wanted a commitment from him that he was
still mourning his first love – a schoolteacher who had died
(Clum 1999: 102). He wrote Edna Ferber agonized letters
about his sexual ambivalence, showing clearly his prime fear
that "he might be unable, finally, to fall in love with anyone at
all, of either sex." He directed his ardor at young, handsome,
blond Glen Boles, confessing to the object of his affection
that "sexuality per se was less important to him than wanting
to love and be loved." Boles quoted him as saying: "If I could
love somebody, I wouldn't care if it was a man, a woman, or a
pig" (Bach 2001: 158).

Of course, bestiality was never on his horizon. What
appeared with great frequency were handsome young men,
though Hart, a devotee of Wilde, was surely sensitive to the

legal and moral issues raised by homosexuality at a time when it was criminalized and condemned in countries (including the United States) that professed to love the sinners they so wholeheartedly denounced. Hart continued to be distressed by the occasional attraction he felt around young actors, especially after he married actress-singer Kitty Carlisle in a simple civil ceremony at Mount Hope, near Fairview Farm, on August 10, 1946, going on to father a son, Christopher (born 1948), and a daughter, Catherine (born 1950). His marriage surprised many of his close friends, especially Irene Selznick, who commented: "We were astonished that Moss wanted to marry and father children, but if that's what he wanted, we were prepared to support him. We had seen Moss from time to time with women – usually just *dogs*. He could have had any girl in the world if he really wanted one, and we all thought – Kitty *Carlisle*?!" (Bach 2001: 270). Selznick's tone betrays a streak of ironic venom, but sweet, ladylike Carlisle was, in fact, the very image of socialite sophistication and glamor. She was always well dressed, immaculately groomed, and with manners that defined social *politesse*. Her outward politeness and perfect etiquette did not necessarily obscure the fact for some observers – such as John Gielgud – that she was beautiful but rather frigid (Gielgud 2004: 260).

Having heard rumours of his bisexuality, Carlisle once asked him: "Are you homosexual?" To which he replied: "Absolutely not!" He mentioned that there had been a couple of men who made passes at him, but that was it (Brown 2006: 268). So, she believed his point-blank denial, even though some of Hart's friends and colleagues were certain that his ambivalence, affectations of speech and manner, advanced stage of bachelorhood, and his friendships with eminent gay men (Cole Porter, Monty Wooley, and Noel Coward) were a sign he was gay (Clum 1999: 102). Celeste Holm, who knew him in the 1940s, believed he was homosexual, but "he didn't want to be" (Brown 2006: 186). In fact, he resorted to psychoanalytic therapy in order to sustain him through periods of despondency and depression occasioned by his sexual ambiguity. Hart discussed his psychoanalysis with Carlisle only in general terms, and she lent a sympathetic ear but never probed (Bach 2001: 268).

The fiction about his heterosexuality is maintained by his biographer, Jared Brown, who quotes Hart's wife: "Moss hated to let me out of his sight. We slept in a double bed, and he wouldn't even let me leave the bed to go in to the children when they were sick" (Brown 2006: 270). Of course, she was not privy to the revelations he made to his psychoanalyst in the matter of his sexuality. Carlisle had admired him from their first meeting, when she felt he was "the best-looking, most arresting man I'd ever seen" (Brown 2006: 112). Seven years younger, she was wise about marital politics, showing (according to their friend Bennett Cerf) "just the right amount of opposition to his most outrageous extravagances before admitting graciously, 'You were absolutely right, Mossie. The room wouldn't look the same without that $600 flower pot in the corner'" (Brown 2006: 271). She allowed him to pick her clothes, jewelry, and perfume so that they would both seem like models of elegance in public, prompting her to remark once: "I felt I was in a continuous drawing-room comedy" (Brown 2006: 208). And she learned to cope with his acute and chronic bouts of depression. When others wondered why he kept going to parties when still depressed, she repeated his explanation: "You don't escape *from* life, you escape *into* it." "He escaped into it so well," she commented, "that no one except me ever knew the effort it cost him" (Brown 2006: 274).

His married life resembled "a flashbulb-lit procession" of dinners, theatre visits, and fashionable parties. However, nothing could squelch his inner disquiet – a condition already reflected in his groundbreaking musical *Lady in the Dark*, co-written with Kurt Weill and Ira Gershwin, starring Gertrude Lawrence. A uniquely hybrid musical play, with episodes from both the real and fantasy lives of the central character (fashion magazine editor Liza Elliott), it refracts Hart's own personal experience with psychoanalysis through Liza. Having fought her way to the top in a man's world, Liza realizes that she is sufficiently unhappy to warrant psychoanalysis that helps her become "well adjusted" at the end. Although this musical was "on the cutting edge of 1941 and sought to address delayed marriage, women in the workplace, and appropriate gender roles for men and women" (McClung 2007: 144), it aged quickly and faded from popularity. But it was a concept musical that incorporated men's changing roles and a masculine persona for Liza in contrast with her feminine dream-self. The character of Russell Paxton, as McClung notes, appears to be "a gay stereotype today," with his effeminate manner, loquaciousness, and attention to clothing, not to mention the fact that he is another Hollywood "eunuch," but Hart was simply drawing on "the prevailing 'invert' profile" (McClung 2007: 149). Homosexual characters were certainly nothing new on Broadway; Mae West had already seen to that. But the New York drama critics usually avoided references to them – at least until the shows were successful.

Some of Moss Hart's associates – particularly Irene Sharaff (costumer for five of his shows) – regarded *Lady in the Dark* as autobiographical (McClung 2007: 152), and Steven Bach suggests that because of his psychosexual issues, Hart began psychoanalysis with Dr. Lawrence (S.) Kubie, who had counseled a number of famous patients, such as Vladimir Horowitz and Tennessee Williams. A critic has suggested that perhaps Russell in the musical "looks back at the unrepressed and evidently unhappy life that Hart was attempting to leave behind, while Liza looks forward to the life that could begin anew once the repressed drive has been brought to light" (McClung 2007: 153).

His inner conflicts sometimes threatened to upset his professional life, though it was a fundamental scepticism about turning *Pygmalion* into a musical that first made him less than amenable to listening to Fritz Loewe's score and Alan Jay Lerner's lyrics for their new project. To begin with, Pascal's suggestion of a musical adaptation had already defeated Rodgers and Hammerstein, and nobody else – from Noel Coward, Cole Porter, and E. Y. Harburg to the team of Arthur Schwartz and Howard Dietz – was willing to make an attempt. So, he did not wish to listen to any of the songs in *My Lady Liza* (as the show was called in its early stages). "It is a fatal enticement," he wrote in explanation in an article years later.

> A composer and a lyricist generally perform their own work with uncommon skill. Too often I have walked resolutely into a meeting with my mind firmly made up, and walked irresolutely out of it, my resolve shaken and my good sense frittered away by an adroit rhyme scheme or a musical phrase of subtlety and charm.
>
> (Brown 2006: 338–9)

But Lerner and Loewe placed enormous pressure on him, and the show had already recruited the services of Harrison, Andrews, Stanley Holloway, Robert Coote, Cecil Beaton, and Oliver Smith. Hart knew that CBS was fully financing the show, and he figured there would be no harm but a great deal of courtesy on his part if he listened politely to the seven completed songs, including "Why Can't the English (Teach Their Children How to Speak)?," "Wouldn't It Be Loverly?," "The Ascot Gavotte," and an early version of "I'm an Ordinary Man." He had been struggling with his own new musical, *In The Pink*, in collaboration with Harold Rome, and he had no new Broadway smash. Besides, his poor health had already led to a heart attack. His initial scepticism began to melt away from the first number. His face took on a peculiar look of surprise, then of almost helpless elation, and after the fourth number, he suddenly exclaimed: "You sons of bitches, I'm hooked!" Later, he reminisced:

> I was uneasily aware that my goose was being cooked. In a few deft lyrical and musical strokes Lerner and Loewe had somehow managed to arrive in the most singular fashion at the correct Shavian attitude – the very attitude I thought it impossible to capture in music and lyrics.
>
> (Brown 2006: 339)

They achieved this despite adding scenes that, in Shaw's play, took place off stage. For example, at the end of the first scene in *Pygmalion*, Eliza returns home, but their musical shows what happens when she does. The elocution lessons, only mentioned in *Pygmalion*, become a dramatic and comic highlight in the musical. Where Alfred P. Doolittle is never seen in his own milieu in Shaw's play, in the musical he has scenes in a pub and on the street, and though he is less of a philosopher in the musical than he is in *Pygmalion*, he is nonetheless a vivid force (Brown 2006: 335–6).

On June 21, 1955 Hart agreed to direct the musical, with his contract calling for a fee of $7,500, plus 3 percent of gross receipts and 6 percent of motion picture rights. He also was to receive a percentage of income from each foreign production (of which there came to be many, from Holland, Belgium, Switzerland, Germany, Sweden, Denmark, Italy, and Spain to Tokyo, Mexico, Israel, Australia, South Africa, and even the Soviet bloc).

When rehearsals began on January 3, 1956, he was back in the New Amsterdam Theatre at 214 West 42nd Street, in a building in which he had begun his career thirty years earlier (Bach 2001: 349). Yet his anxiety and insomnia only worsened to the point where he needed tranquilizers, which his psychoanalyst had wanted to deny him. He nevertheless returned to theatre work with a new focus and determination, bent on determining the emotional and dramatic heart of the musical. He identified it in Eliza's on-stage transformation from flower girl to Cinderella literally on her way to the Embassy Ball. He decided that her preparations for the ball should form the climax at the end of Act I, so that the audience would be in some suspense and anticipation after the intermission.

What Hart may not even have been aware of at the time was his consolidation of and challenge to Julie Andrews's image as a woman. Andrews was fully persuasive as a Cinderella figure, and she was always the epitome of British composure and grace. But in *My Fair Lady*, she would be part of a heterosexual romantic relationship that was unpersuasive to some critics and a violation of Shaw's didactic logic. The world of *My Fair Lady* was dominated by male characters: Higgins, Colonel Pickering, Alfred P. Doolittle and his pub chums, and, to a lesser extent (but crucial to the plot), Zoltan Karpathy. Yet Hart must surely have noticed the gay codes in the material, especially through all the references to Higgins and Pickering's being confirmed bachelors, rather like some of Wilde's epicene dandies. If it is an exaggeration to call the situation homosexual, it is certainly fair to call it "homosocial," as Stacy Wolf does (Wolf 2002: 152), though I prefer to spell it "homo-social." Borrowing Eve Kosofsky Sedgwick's theory of triangulation, Wolf illuminates the central, developing relationship of Higgins and Pickering in order to reveal how this "homo-sociality" delightfully undoes "heterosexual presumption" (Wolf 2002: 152), despite, I would add, the machismo of Rex Harrison and the chaste femininity of Julie Andrews.

4

"Why can't a woman be more like a man?"

At the first full reading, everyone was understandably keyed up so that the atmosphere was electric. "Each number was spontaneously applauded," according to Cecil Beaton (Beaton 1976: 39). Rex Harrison plunged into his role with the sort of excitement that turned the reading into what Moss Hart memorialized as "a thing to be set apart and remembered with gratitude," just as with Gertrude Lawrence at the first reading of *Lady in the Dark* (Hart 1959: 312). Lerner's recollection was different – at least of the second act, when, contrary to the continuing enthusiasm of the rest of the cast, Harrison's face "grew longer and longer and his voice softer and softer" because Higgins had "gotten lost in the second act" (Lerner 1978: 92).

On the way to a dinner engagement with Harrison at the Hotel Pierre that evening, Lerner thought back to a week earlier when the two men, while strolling down Fifth Avenue, had reviewed their respective sorry marital difficulties. Harrison had suddenly stopped and said in a loud voice that attracted public attention: "Alan! Wouldn't it be marvellous if we were homosexuals?" This was remarkably out of character for an actor reputed to be homophobic and a real ladies' man, and although Lerner dismissed the idea, he must have revolved the comment in his mind. When the two men walked back to the Hotel Pierre, "still discussing women," they found Nancy Olson (Lerner's wife at the time) in a terrible temper, awaiting her tardy husband. She was having difficulties with Lerner's being a workaholic, "who preferred to spend his evenings working with the boys rather than being with her." When Lerner attempted to stifle her angry interruptions of his conversation with Harrison, she suddenly declared bitterly: "What you really mean, Alan, is why can't a woman be more like a man." Lerner raced to his desk and created "A Hymn to Him" (commonly known as "Why Can't a Woman Be More like a Man?") (Harrison 1991: 138–9). Lerner himself felt that the song "seemed a perfect second act vehicle through which Higgins could release his rage against Eliza for leaving him" (Lerner 1978: 92). But it was also a number that underwent several revisions before the final version.

Harrison reverted to his alpha-male self, which remained a problem throughout rehearsals and try-outs, but his immense comedic talent and vocal technique offset his impatience and egotistical outbursts. Julie Andrews, however, was clearly out of her depth. Moss Hart met her for the first time at rehearsal, and found her charming but clueless about her part. By the fifth day, he was really terrified that she was not going to survive. Andrews knew what she wanted, but every time she tried to do it, as she complained to friends, "something comes up in front of me and I'm like a crab clawing at a glass wall with Moss on the other side" (Windeler 1983: 27). She had no idea how to do a cockney accent, so Alfred Dixon was hired as her dialect coach in a delectable irony of an English actress taking cockney lessons from an American professor of phonetics – her own Henry Higgins, as she notes in her memoir! – only to have her stage Higgins instruct her in how to speak properly without that accent (Andrews 2008: 191). She had already sensed from a meeting with Lerner, Loewe, and Harrison that her leading man had "a clear sense of himself, albeit somewhat egocentric." Her description of her leading man is diplomatic, to say the least, though she also notes that he was "definitely the center of attention" (Andrews 2008: 188). She irritated Harrison with her disconcerting habit of walking into the theatre while practicing scales at top voice and with her clumsy acting. She also had a nervous habit of laughing in his face during dramatic scenes. Harrison interpreted her reaction as one of bemusement at his interpretation, and although he lies about the harmony he enjoyed with her during the full run of the show ("in the three years we played together we never had a cross word of any kind" [Harrison 1975: 162]), he once stormed out of rehearsals, threatening: "If that girl is here on Monday giving the same goddamn performance, I'm out of this show" (Bach 2001: 355). Only he probably said "cunt" instead of "girl" – as was reported years later to Andrews (Andrews 2008: 194).

It was eminently clear to Hart that something drastic needed to be done with her. At 20, she was a veteran and a trouper but unusually shy for a performer, and though she moved with grace, and had immaculate diction and an enviably flexible soprano, she was nowhere near the role as Eliza, and therefore far from the shadows of Mrs. Patrick Campbell, Lynn Fontanne, Wendy Hiller, and Gertrude Lawrence, who had all played Eliza to acclaim. Hart vented his frustration to his wife, who advised him to take Andrews to a hotel for the weekend: "I'd never let her out; I'd order up room service. I'd keep her there and *paste* the part on her." He reminded Andrews that this was "stolen time" he couldn't really afford, so there could be no time for politeness and she must not take offence because there are no "second chances in the theatre. There isn't time to sit down and do the whole Actors' Studio bit. We have to start from the first line and go over the play line by line" (Bach 2001: 355–6). To her credit, she understood perfectly, though she felt as if she was at the dentist "to have a tooth pulled." He put her on a rigorous regimen that required long rehearsals of some seven hours daily, excluding a short meal break. He could be blunt: "You're playing this like a Girl Guide," "You're not thinking, you're just oozing out the scene," or "You're too light, much too light." Lerner's production assistant, Stone "Bud" Widney attested: "He dirtied her up. There are two parts to Eliza: one she's a scruffy little street urchin and then she becomes a lady and while Julie was practicing the lady, she forgot the urchin" (Bach 2001: 357). Hart was Henry Higgins in reverse, using cockney-isms he had once heard from his father in childhood, but it was necessary to get her to hear what Eliza should sound like. For two days, Moss and she "hammered through each scene – everything from Eliza's entrance, her screaming and yelling, to her transformation into a lady at the end of the play. Moss bullied, cajoled, scolded, and encouraged." By the end of the forty-eight hours, he had stripped her feelings bare, and disposed of her "girlish inadequacy; he had molded, kneaded, and helped [her] become the character of Eliza" (Andrews 2008: 196). Later, Hart would remark: "We were both absolutely done in, exhausted. But she made it. She has that terrible English strength that makes you wonder why they lost India" (Bach

2001: 357). When she reported for rehearsals again with the company, Harrison exclaimed: "My goodness, Julie, you *have* improved." Kitty Carlisle Hart found that while listening to her after ten days, she "could hear every inflection of Moss's," and as rehearsals progressed, Kitty couldn't take her eyes off her. "She mowed everything down with her charm" (Stirling 2007: 77).

Although Hart kept the company in good spirits with fresh jokes and a daily tea break for the British contingent, he could not quell Harrison's egotism. In a later memoir, Harrison admitted to feeling under duress by the very fact of risking his considerable reputation "for a certain, very particular kind of comic acting, to do something [he] didn't know [he] could do" (Harrison 1991: 124). He annoyed Cecil Beaton with his excessive complaints about minute details of costuming, prompting Beaton, an acid, egotistical dandy in his own right, to remark that Harrison was "like a dog with a rat" and would "worry" details at great length. If given the opportunity, Harrison would work himself up into a state of nervous alarm, and was therefore not "the easiest boy in the class" (Beaton 1976: 37–8). But Beaton had his own egotistical issues – he was reluctant to work in tandem with Oliver Smith (the scenic designer) because he vowed to "never again participate in only one of the facets of what I considered should be a visual whole" (Beaton 1976: 37) – his diaries (written with a poison pen, no doubt) record Harrison's tantrums, indecisions, and doubts. One morning, Harrison ripped off his first-act long coat in anger because it was tight under the arms. "The seams split and the expensive stuff was frayed. The 'strait-jacket' was thrown to the floor." Then, one evening after dinner at Beaton's, the actor suddenly decided he did not want to play the role of Higgins. "They wanted Gielgud – they'd better get him." In a panic, Beaton telephoned New York and Harrison soon changed his mind (Beaton 1976: 38). This ego exercise betrayed a deep-rooted fear of failure. Harrison would rehearse his lyrics so often that the rest of the company was worn down. The chorus girls lay on the floor or sprawled in the stalls, while Harrison repeated, over and over, certain phrases of "I've Grown Accustomed to Her Face." At length, when he was playing the last-act quarrel scene with Eliza and she threw the slippers hard in his face, the entire chorus applauded from the stalls (Beaton 1976: 39–40). Beaton, however, did side with Harrison over his perfectionist attitude: "No doubt Rex was right. He knew his performance was more important than the impatience of thirty chorus-girls and dancers." But there were times when the actor's "continuing egotism" upset him to such an extent that "only by a miracle" was Beaton prevented from "making an ugly scene."

Harrison's perfectionism was linked to severe insecurity. Knowing full well that his singing voice was not up to par for the score, he visited a maestro in Wigmore Street who taught *bel canto*, which proved to be an error, for the maestro seemed to want Harrison to "become an Italian and roar through the window, and try to hit [a] house across the street" with his voice (Harrison 1991: 132–3). Three visits were enough to convince him that he would never be a singer, "not in the accepted sense of the word," so Lerner referred him to Bill Lowe,[1] who conducted the orchestra in the pit at the London Coliseum. At the piano installed in his hotel suite, Harrison

---

1 Where Lerner and Harrison both refer to a Bill Lowe, McHugh (2012) mentions a Roy Lowe.

worked with Lowe, who advised him not to think about singing the words but to start by just saying them

> There is such a thing as talking on pitch – using only
> those notes that you want to use, picking them out of
> the score, sometimes more, sometimes less. For the rest of
> the time, concentrate on staying on pitch, even though
> you're only speaking.
>
> (Harrison 1975: 157)

It was an old-fashioned method, well known to English
music-hall performers, but the advice was a revelation to
Harrison, who took it to heart and thereby created the
Sprechgesang style he would use in *My Fair Lady*, a style in
which words were spoken to the rhythm of a tune (157).
As Harrison once wrote of this: "It's an old and evocative
form, and you get much more meaning into words when you
use the music as underscoring than singers can do when they
sing them. This is because you can give full weight and true
expression to them. With ordinary singing, especially opera
singing, you're thinking much more of the noise you're making. You can't give words and music equal weight, you see, that's
the trouble" (Harrison 1991: 135). Harrison had no trouble
staying on pitch and singing or talking right in the middle
of the note. Louis "Satchmo" Armstrong complimented him
months later at the Mark Hellinger Theatre: "You're hitting
every note right down the middle" (Harrison 1991: 133).
As one of his subsequent directors remarked, Harrison's sinu-
ous stage speaking voice produced its own "eloquent music"
with "the swoops and barks and sudden, heart-stopping plunge
of his tone, and the pantherine grace of his half-pouncing,
half-floating walk which ploughed such furrows in feminine

hearts – even though, much of the time they were unaware of it" (Garland 1998: 36).

Besides worrying about the correct way of delivering the song lyrics, he also wanted to be true to Shaw – a playwright he claims he would eventually spend a good half of his life performing[2] – and his chief worry at the beginning of the enterprise was that the lyrics would not match Shaw's dialogue in *Pygmalion*. So, he zealously carried around a Penguin edition of *Pygmalion* in his pocket, consulting it frequently and interrupting Hart to argue every point. He appeared to have become Henry Higgins, intent on defending the English language against "barbaric" Americans. After enduring his frequent interruptions and cries of "Where's my Penguin?," Lerner bought a stuffed penguin from a taxidermist, and the next time Harrison cried out "Where's my Penguin?" the stuffed bird was rolled out on to the stage, cracking up everyone, including Harrison. "From that moment on, he never mentioned the Penguin again and kept the stuffed edition in his dressing room as a mascot throughout the run of the production" (Lerner 1978: 93–5). By his own admission, Lerner did make "one grave error." When Harrison marveled at one of Higgins's speeches after the "Rain in Spain" number and asked him: "Where in Shaw did you find it?," Lerner confessed: "I wrote it." Harrison suddenly lost respect for the passage and seldom got it right in rehearsal. Ever after, if Harrison inquired of a line "Is that yours?," Lerner would

2 Harrison acted in *Major Barbara*, *Caesar and Cleopatra*, and *Heartbreak House* – which hardly substantiates his claim, though his critical success as Shotover and his long runs as Higgins add considerably to his expertise in Shaw.

always claim to have found it somewhere in Shaw's writings – perhaps in "one of Shaw's letters or in a preface or an essay" (Lerner 1978: 95–6).

Harrison impressed on Lerner and Loewe that they needed to write songs for him that could be spoken rather than sung flat out. The first one they tried was the introductory book-number "Why Can't the English Teach Their Children How to Speak?" because it mirrored the opening line of Shaw's stage play: "Every time an Englishman opens his mouth, another Englishman despises him." However, Harrison felt that the first version of the song didn't work very well because "at the beginning it was just a statement of Higgins's intellectual position – until they injected into it all the anger and frustration he would feel." Once the pair cottoned on to the idea that he needed an emotional foundation from which to speak rather than sing, things improved – especially after he let it be known that he didn't want to sound "like an inferior Noel Coward" (Harrison 1991: 119). Lerner felt the initial problem might have been the rhyme scheme, which made Harrison feel that it resembled Coward's "Mad Dogs and Englishmen." So he set about breaking it down and changing it right through rehearsals, promising the actor (in a letter on November 29, 1955) that he would "rewrite it completely in a way that will be not only simpatico with you, but with the character of Higgins" (McHugh 2012: 135). Lerner realized that he needed to change the number from what he called "a song-song" full of "satiric extravagance" to a "character song" that was "broader in scope and a longer line musically" and that would be accompanied by emotions.

Towards the second week of rehearsal, the musical found its title. Herman Levin's layout for the first newspaper advertisement in New Haven, Connecticut, began: "Herman Levin

Presents Rex Harrison and Julie Andrews in ?" Levin made an urgent appeal for a working title. Early suggestions of *Liza* and *My Lady Liza* "went to their final resting places in the trash basket." Lerner suggested that the title should be a compromise – "the title that we all dislike the least." There was "a collective, apathetic nod," and the compromise title was *My Fair Lady*, despite Frederick Loewe's preference for *Fanfaroon* (a rarely used word meaning someone who blows his own horn) (Lerner 1978: 79, 98). Harrison approved of the title because the possessive "My" stressed "the dominating masculine angle," and the phrase itself (from the children's song "London Bridge Is Falling Down") was "a pun, in the cockney accent, on Mayfair Lady, which Eliza wasn't, and Higgins made her seem" (Harrison 1991: 116).

Rex Harrison raised another controversy before the New Haven opening when he made it clear that he was not going to stand up on stage "like an idiot doing nothing" while Julie Andrews sang "Without You." He did not object to the song or its content – Eliza's triumphant liberation from Higgins – but he felt upstaged and foolishly immobile. Lerner and Loewe panicked, but Moss Hart remained calm, deciding to do nothing until everything else in the play was rehearsed. As biographer Jared Brown remarks, he was unlike the stereotype of the loud, dictatorial director "who races about, nerves jangling, shouting at actors and technicians, periodically giving ways to fits of temperament." Instead, he was "quiet, methodical, reasonable, thorough, infinitely patient, never undercutting an actor's self-confidence, never fighting to establish his supremacy over other members of the production team" (Brown 2006: 244). On the train to New Haven, Hart informed Harrison that Andrews was going to sing "Without You" whether he was on stage or not. "It is my personal opinion you will look like a horse's ass if you leave the stage when she begins it and return when she has finished. However, if you will give me the opportunity, I will show you how it can be staged." No more was said, and Harrison kept his place on stage at the very first New Haven rehearsal at the Shubert Theatre. He didn't want to be a horse's ass and he realized that Hart, Lerner, and Loewe planned for Higgins to interrupt the song at its climax with: "I did it. I did it. I said I'd make a woman and indeed I did" (Lerner 1978: 101). His interruption reaffirmed his Pygmalian arrogance, and deflected attention away from her ecstasy to his own chauvinistic rhyming brio. The repetitive phrases, set in a brisk staccato of consonance, allowed his dynamism and sharp assertiveness to top her celebration. And the quick tempo recalled the tango rhythm of "The Rain in Spain," where Eliza was spontaneously and briefly allowed to be an equal partner with Higgins and Pickering at a peak of sheer blissful accomplishment.

Julie Andrews tried to be encouraging about the orchestral accompaniment by saying: "Just wait until you get the orchestra. It's like a marvellous sort of eiderdown you can relax into" (Harrison 1975: 163). That was true if you were a genuine singer, but he was a song-speaker. But Franz Allers had a full orchestra with thirty-two musicians and Rex had only been used to a rehearsal pianist. He heard a cacophony from the pit and exploded at Allers (in a scene that is preserved for documentary posterity on videotape at the New York Public Library at Lincoln Center), demanding that the orchestra stop and redo the orchestrations before he would sing another note. Hart rehearsed him alone with the musicians, and Allers designated a clarinet in the pit to carry the melody for Harrison from beginning to end of the performance (Bach 2001: 358–9). But on opening night, February 4, a blizzard raged. The performance was sold out but Harrison, paralyzed with fear, refused to go on. His New York agent, David Hocker, was pale, but, grasping the seriousness of the situation, informed his client that "he was never likely to work again if word got out, and that he would personally see to it that word got out." Harrison reneged, but not before spreading his own panic to Robert Coote (Pickering), who turned into "a basket case" (Bach 2001: 359).

The upshot of the experience was the swelling roar of enthusiastic approval by the opening-night audience, especially after the "Rain in Spain" number. The cheering, laughing, screaming, and stomping brought the show to a halt, and Harrison and Coote were dumbfounded. But Andrews grabbed them and dragged them to the apron of the stage, where she led them in bows until the ovation subsided and allowed the show to continue.

In time, Andrews's relationship with Harrison did change into something relatively amicable. True to form, she was, in retrospect, full of compliments about him:

> He was quirky, selfish, charming, dashing and brilliant – and I would learn so much, just by standing on stage and watching him. However mad one got at him for the odd bit of selfishness, he cut the mustard every night so brilliantly that one forgave him.
>
> (Stirling 2007: 90)

Harrison, in turn, praised her: "She is marvellously even, her performance doesn't vary; it is highly professional from the word Go. Julie always was – a very boring old word – a good trouper" (Stirling 2007: 90). His carefully worded compliment barely conceals a tiny residue of equivocation.

Sophisticated performer though he was, Harrison could never erase his egotism, which grew worse two years later in London when he decided that he had already triumphed as Henry Higgins and did not require any more of Moss Hart's direction – or rehearsals with Julie Andrews – or with anyone else, including the new members of the English cast. When informed by Hart in front of the company that he was required to rehearse along with everyone else, Harrison exploded: "You Jewish cunt! If it hadn't been for me you would never have got this job directing the show in the first place." A two-hour confrontation ensued, hectic with screaming invective overheard by stunned wives waiting in the next room to go out to dinner. The only abuse Harrison neglected to utter – though he did later in England – was to call Franz Allers "that Nazi in the pit" (Garland 1998: 27). Finally, Binkie Beaumont (the London impresario) told Harrison he would be happily replaced by Michael Redgrave or John Gielgud. Refusing to yield his primacy in musical comedy to either of those knights – he was "the incomparable Rex," after all – he agreed to rehearse (Bach 2001: 361), with nary a complaint – till his next anticipated explosion. However, the London version showed that Harrison could no longer dominate everything and everyone on stage. The *Daily Telegraph* said approvingly: "Julie Andrews's Eliza seems to me to have gained in force and fire," while Kenneth Tynan in the *Observer* was more colorfully enthusiastic: "Nothing in Julie Andrews' cockney becomes her like the leaving of it, but she blossoms once she has shed her fraudulent accent, into a first-rate Eliza, with a voice as limpid as outer space" (Stirling 2007: 94–5). Her confidence and newfound experience reconfigured the show, and as Drew Middleton wrote in his *New York Times* review of May 4, 1958:

Eliza Doolittle is a more mature, commanding and subtle performance here. In New York Rex Harrison's near
miraculous playing as Henry Higgins seemed to throw
the musical slightly out of balance. In London Miss
Andrews has redressed the balance.

Twenty-three years later, director Patrick Garland discovered that Harrison was "frequently at his least charitable when
talking about his fellow artists, in particular whoever played
Eliza Doolittle." When informed that a young English singer
who auditioned for the show had been Andrews's under-
study, looked just like her, and had a natural singing voice,
Harrison countered that that was exactly what he didn't
want. He didn't want anyone looking or talking like Audrey
Hepburn or Andrews. He felt that the only true Eliza would
be "a real London girl, a cockney, and much tougher than the
earlier Elizas" because he wanted a challenge as Higgins: "By
making her tougher and rougher, so to speak, it would be
more difficult for Higgins to turn her into a lady" (Harrison
1991: 216). Garland believed that Harrison was disingenuous,
in that he was "essentially uninterested in a perfect Eliza . . .
Whatever fuss was made about Miss Doolittle was pointless,
because nobody was interested in the girl. They were only
interested in *him*" (Garland 1998: 59). And Harrison never
forgot the fact that he had considerable sex appeal for women.
The only actress who won his heart (briefly) as Eliza was
reputedly Cheryl Kennedy, whom Patrick Garland describes
as "a young woman with a natural cockney lilt to her voice,
as well as a poignant beauty, fitting for a Duchess" (Garland
1998: 116). When she was forced to leave the production
because of nodes on her vocal cords, her successor, Nancy
Ringham, immediately became the target of Harrison's

disapproval. He deflated her so completely that her performance was lifeless. On one occasion, when she yelled out at Ascot: "Come on, Dover, move your bloomin' arse!" as the curtain fell, Harrison hissed in her ear, clutching a copy of *Sporting Life*: "I'd like to stick this up your blooming arse!" (Garland 1998: 197–8).

Ned Sherrin (English writer, broadcaster, director, and producer) had an ingenious theory about Harrison, explaining that his curious (and often cruel) way of rejecting dozens of potential Elizas was his way of pursuing an imaginary Eliza inside his head, and that this habitual rejection of a candidate and of choreography were devices for him to recreate the role of Henry Higgins in a fresh way, though he ended up doing the role exactly as he had done it years before (Garland 1998: 79). Harrison had an unshakable view that Eliza was too often wrongly played by elegant actresses struggling to speak stage-cockney, instead of being a cockney girl struggling to break into middle-class speech and rank. Harrison was fond of repeating his mantra: "Eliza is the same girl, right the way through, she is the same character, the same spirit, in the first scene in Covent Garden, as she is in the last scene with Henry's mother." He maintained that her streak of coarseness and danger, which threatened to snap and make an ass of her, was exactly what Higgins (and Shaw) fall in love with (Garland 1998: 80).

Was it just a matter of Higgins's being jealous of Eliza, or was it simply a case of Rex Harrison not wishing to share the limelight with his fair lady? This musical is not a one-man show, though Harrison always attempted to make it so. When Cheryl Kennedy (whom he *briefly* admired in the role) completed her performance in a run-through in New York, Harrison was furious because, as he explained, what she dared do was "suddenly come forward and give a performance, which was a) good and b) threatened to dominate me" (Garland 1998: 144). He later attempted to justify his attitude: "My instincts, naturally, are invariably right, and when I feel something's wrong, I damn well know it *is* wrong. And I don't want to stand up there, looking like a c★★t" (Garland 1998: 144). He was perfectly oblivious to the fact that his tyrannical desire for absolute control took all the fun out of a production. The "c" word – one of his favorite swear words – was usually employed as a synonym for "cretin" or "moron" or "arsehole," and most of the time it was directed towards men rather than women. In fact, he often used it against himself – as when he described the investiture ceremony of his knighthood in the summer of 1989. Miffed at the fact that the Queen wasn't properly briefed and, so, did not remember who he was, he nevertheless felt that the occasion had gone off reasonably well: "Mind you, you'd have to be a complete c★★t *not* to get it right – !" (Garland 1998: 208).

Harrison seemed to prefer not to see *My Fair Lady* as a musical with three leading characters: Higgins, Doolittle, and Eliza. His male chauvinism insisted on dominating everyone and everything, leading Patrick Garland to wonder how Harrison managed to agree to "so obviously feminine a title. He would have settled for 'My Fair Professor Higgins' no doubt" (Garland 1998: 206). But even though he always strove to make it a one-man or two-man show, Harrison could not fight off the feminist implications of Shaw's play or the musical.

5

Queer meanings

The evidence is clear: the original production of *My Fair Lady* had an alpha-male Henry Higgins, who believed the show was really about him, and that Eliza was merely a device of Shaw's to contrast Higgins's intellectual, social, and linguistic superiority with her "guttersnipe" inferiority – until the Pygmalion or Svengali or Prince ("Uncharming") worked his magic on her and transformed her into a consort worthy of him. The Eliza was a chaste virginal sort, a thoroughly English diva in the making, who required someone like this Higgins in order to liberate her from all others of his type, until such time as she was able to find an equal footing with him. And the "magician" behind the scenes who made the fairy-tale musical reach its apogee on stage was a sexually ambiguous and anguished American (with English bloodlines) who was a Pygmalion of sorts himself, taking the very young English Galatea and showing her a way of surviving and then transcending her stage Pygmalion. This was not, of course, the whole meaning of the musical, but it certainly was something more profound than the interpretations formulated by some critics.

Henry Higgins puts soul before language when he chides Eliza, though his soul lacks any spark except of rhetoric: "Remember that you are a human being with a soul and the divine gift of articulate speech . . ." (Lerner 1956: 26–7). The problem with Higgins is that his soul is obscured by his virtuosic rhetoric, which Harrison turned into a stunning symphony – as described by Patrick Garland in his memoir *The Incomparable Rex* – and bettered by no other successor in the role, not even Ian Richardson, Jonathan Pryce, or Canada's Colm Feore, each of whom was a Higgins of considerable merit. Harrison was virtually an entire orchestra in his cautionary to Eliza, starting with, "Eliza, you are to live here for the next six months, learning to speak beautifully, like a lady in a florist's shop" (Lerner 1956: 54), which he spoke with extreme tenderness and courtesy one minute before becoming threatening, dropping a full octave, then launching his voice "into a magnificent series of arabesques," encompassing a machine-gun staccato, a rising scale, "a pause of utter sweetness, and then descending with infinite grace, down, down to his lowest register, concluding almost with a swoon – 'and the angels will *weep* for you'" (Garland 1998: 168).

Sharing André Previn's belief that *My Fair Lady* is "the perfect musical play" is to be blissfully unaware of some of the limitations in Lerner's lyrics – flaws such as the grammatically problematic lyric in "I'm an Ordinary Man": "I'd be equally as willing / For a dentist to be drilling / Than to ever let a woman in my life," or the imperfect rhyme ("bother me" and "rather be") in "On the Street where You Live." Moreover, Higgins and Eliza are more layered in *Pygmalion* than they are in *My Fair Lady*. One of the qualities that Canadian critic Mark Steyn identifies in *My Fair Lady* is its "author-power," by which he probably means its literary source: George Bernard

Shaw (Steyn 2000: 265). He also could be referring to Alan J. Lerner, who, he claims, was not so far way "from the urbane, charming misogyny of Henry Higgins" (Steyn 2000: 285).

In terms of dialogue, *My Fair Lady* is remarkably faithful to Shaw's original, so much so that it could play well even without its music. It is also true that Lerner and Loewe created music that "moved it away from Shaw's conception and closer to what its casts and audiences had always been predisposed to take it for: a version of *Cinderella*" (Knapp 2006: 285). Yet there are profound differences between *Cinderella* and *My Fair Lady*, not the least of which is that *Cinderella* is *her* story, whereas *My Fair Lady* is usually read as *his* story, perhaps because of Higgins's seemingly indomitable authority and Harrison's singular stamp on the role.

Raymond Knapp points out how the musical adds an intriguingly ironic twist to the Pygmalion–Galatea legend. There is a hint of incest to Galatea's union because Pygmalion is her sculptor-father with whom she unites. In *My Fair Lady*, there is a whiff of something unsavory in the shared domestic situation of Higgins and Pickering, two "confirmed old bachelors," and in Higgins's "frequently expressed contempt for women." The sexual implications are strong: Higgins and Pickering are either homosexual or buddies, which is to say that they express sexual repression:

> Higgins's possible homosexuality must be understood in relation to a developmental trope particularly common in England, in which homosexual relations are understood to be a phase within a longer process of a young male's maturation into a normal heterosexual man. Higgins thus becomes a case of arrested development.
>
> (Knapp 2006: 286)

The point is borne out in his mother's rebuke of him and Pickering: "You certainly are a pretty pair of babies, playing with your live doll" (Lerner 1956: 101). Knapp also offers into comic evidence Higgins's collection of Japanese dresses ready for Eliza to wear, and Higgins's quick knowledge of where to buy ladies' gowns. There is also a scene in which Pickering serves as a dressmaker's dummy for Eliza's new gown.

So, the relationships within the musical are crucially important as far as the manufacture of meaning is concerned. Reviews of the original Broadway production are divided on the Eliza–Higgins relationship, with Brooks Atkinson, Robert Coleman, and John McClain all stressing a romantic angle, while William Hawkins, John Chapman, Walter Kerr, and Richard Watts, Jr. make no comment on the subject (McHugh 2012: 172). After Atkinson's revisiting the show, his new review refers to romance but appears "to backtrack from his firm portrayal of the supposed love between Eliza and Higgins." He acknowledges the fact that "the hero and heroine never kiss," and that *My Fair Lady* "reflects Shaw's lack of interest in the stage ritual of sex" (McHugh 2012: 172). There is no physical confirmation of their love, "surely a stumbling block for anyone who wants to read the final reunion of Eliza and Higgins as a capitulation to conventional romantic 'happy endings'" (McHugh 2012: 202).

Is the happy romantic ending implied? Shaw subtitled *Pygmalion* "A Romance," but made it clear in the section entitled "Sequel" in the 1916 edition of the play that the subtitle referred to the "transfiguration of Eliza and not to a union between her and Higgins." Shaw acknowledged that this transfiguration was "exceedingly improbable," but also cited historical precedents "of resolutely ambitious young women" since Nell Gwynne's time. He found it "unbearable" that people "have assumed, for no other reason than that she became the heroine of a romance, that she must have married the hero of it." Shaw insisted that in telling Higgins she would not marry him, Eliza was announcing "a well-considered decision." Her instincts were telling her not to marry, but this does not mean that he would not remain "one of the strongest personal interests in her life." She seems to understand intuitively that Higgins lacks the makings of a husband. He has a passion for phonetics rather than people, and he idealizes his mother rather than Eliza (Shaw 1962: 281–3). She is drawn to Freddy Eynsford-Hill because he pours out his love for her daily through the post, is:

> practically twenty years younger than Higgins: he is a gentleman (or, as Eliza would qualify him, a toff), and speaks like one; he is nicely dressed, is treated by the Colonel as an equal, loves her unaffectedly, and is not her master, nor ever likely to dominate her in spite of his advantage of social standing.

Eliza rejects "the foolish romantic tradition that all women love to be mastered, if not actually bullied and beaten." So, her choice is between a lifetime of fetching Higgins's slippers or a lifetime of Freddy fetching hers (Shaw 1962: 284–5). "In other words," concludes Dominic McHugh, "Eliza's unlikely rise through the social ranks is the romantic element of the plot, rather than the romance itself" (McHugh 2012: 51).

But there are subtleties in *My Fair Lady* that, perhaps, were never envisaged by Shaw. Harrison-Higgins could always talk but not sing, whereas Andrews-Eliza could always sing but not talk. As Ethan Mordden has described, Eliza has several "warring vocal registers" as she transforms from the cockney guttersnipe to the beautiful debutante, and Andrews had to negotiate all these registers adeptly, with an ever-present threat to her own voice. The genius of the musical (to repeat what Raymond Knapp takes from Rick Altman) is to indicate that each of these characters, Higgins and Eliza, is "double, made up of both a surface and a repressed personality," and that the surface personality of each corresponds to the repressed personality of the other (Knapp 2006: 289). Higgins (through Harrison's performance) is the well-bred English gentleman. Whether in pullover, tweed, or tails, he is expressly non-hirsute. In fact, his receding hairline, with hair swept back at the temples, could be read as a sign of genteel maturity, a civilized sensuality. His Higgins "longs for a musical lyricism (that is, figuratively, and expressible emotionality) as deeply as Eliza longs for Higgins's locutionary skills (and empowering reason)" (Knapp 2006: 289). In the 1956 Broadway version (as Stacy Wolf has shown), Julie Andrews provided "both the 'Cinderella' identity known to mainstream America and a more challenging, even feminist and queer kind of woman" (Wolf 2002: 142). When Eliza walks out of Higgins's home, her life is really beginning, whereas Higgins seems too attached to his mother to have any capacity for romance or self-knowledge. It can also be argued that Rex Harrison provided both the Pygmalion identity known to legend and a more challenging, queer type of man. And both were guided along the way by a director who was queer in his own particular way, as I have indicated in an earlier chapter.

Clearly, *My Fair Lady* shows that both Eliza and Higgins learn from each other, though in almost every production the relationship is from Higgins's perspective. In challenging this perspective, more recent productions have tended to sharpen the question of where Eliza fits into Shaw's heterosexual triangulation of Higgins, Pickering, and Eliza. She discovers near the end that she cannot really go back home again, because when she returns briefly to the Covent Garden flower market, she is not at first recognized by her former cohorts. She is displaced by her own transformation.

There is no love song for Eliza; only Freddy sings of love or of being enamored by her, but his song (a soliloquy) is situated outside her bedroom in Wimpole Street ("On the Street where You Live"), and it expresses a desire for a *princesse lointaine*, because although Eliza is so very nearby, she is, in another sense, so far away: "And oh! the towering feeling / Just to know somehow you are near! / The overpowering feeling / That any second you may suddenly appear" (Lerner 1956: 111). There is no denying the fact that the song generates uncomfortable questions about Freddy's character and his worthiness as a foil to Higgins. Part of his lyric is pure romance; part stamps him as the butt of comedy – a serenading fool, quite overpowered by feeling. It is a tribute to Eliza, who does not know about his absolute devotion to her, and its surcharged feeling seems right out of a fairy tale or courtly myth. But is it right in context or is it a misfit, despite its becoming a worldwide hit on pop charts? The evidence is weighted more on the side of its being something that has suddenly appeared almost out of nowhere rather than being properly integrated.

The first act devotes three songs to Higgins – two of which could be generally classified as solos (with some choral cueing) – and four to Eliza – three of which are essentially solos. That Eliza has more songs than Higgins is probably caused by the fact that she is the title character who causes essential change in her antagonist as well as in herself. A simpler reason could be the fact that the role calls for a soprano

voice that complements Freddy's tenor and offsets the patter and/or vaudevillian quality of Higgins's and Doolittle's
songs. Moreover, true to Shaw's dialectic, the songs of Eliza
and Higgins crystallize the linguistic, social, and psychological
conflicts between the professor-autocrat and his naive but
vital pupil. Her songs express a hopeful optimism. Dominic
McHugh contends that they define her as "the ultimate
Broadway musical heroine" because "from start to finish she
embodies the triumph of aspiration as well as being a representative of feminism, women's suffrage, and social mobility"
(McHugh 2012: 201). In addition to wanting to be warm
and comfortable, she has ambition, and her goal of becoming
"a lady in a flower shop" speaks to an aspect of social mobility. She declares her independence in the feisty "Without
You," and demands "something more than empty promises in
'Show Me'" (McHugh 2012: 201). The latter song has a Latin
flavor, "a bit like the *huagpango* that Bernstein was later to
use for 'America' in *West Side Story* but without any obvious
intention of evoking the exotic." Lerner and Loewe's com-
position is dazzling in its projection of Eliza's fury through
multiple meters, lines of longer syllabication, and diction that
is colloquial where the tension of the piece is communicated
by "dense harmonies and the imperative tense (such as 'Don't,'
'Read,' and 'Tell')" (McHugh 2012: 132). And, honoring her
talent, Julie Andrews was able to take the solo in her stride –
with Freddy's bewildered attempt to articulate his ardor for
her interrupted by her violent dissatisfaction and disgust with
mere words. She already gets enough words, in the most
unromantic way, from Higgins, her tutor, so she hardly needs
Freddy's. To echo Eric Bentley, where Higgins spoke to keep
his domination over her, she talked to free herself (Bentley
1957: 120). So, she is done with words, and she asserts her

potent will, stifling Freddy's soft, dreamy romanticism: in the process, she suggests how he is an unworthy suitor because he is unable to match her force of personality, and, new woman that she is, she even resorts to grabbing and "fairly" flinging him down the street.

Intriguingly, the lyrics and the actress's rendition of them forge an alignment between Andrews and Mary Martin in the sense of feminine and lesbian tropes. Martin's tomboy trope came to the fore in *South Pacific*, where, as Nellie Forbush, she would rather be "butch" than play the girl, and in parts of *The Sound of Music*, where she frolicked with the children and stood up to their father. So, when Andrews came to play Maria in the film version of *The Sound of Music* (where she looked younger and more attractive than Martin's governess), she likewise repeated the same trope, rushing back to the convent from the mountains like a tornado, engaging in pillow-fights with Von Trapp's children, bicycling, and romping with them in the countryside. Andrews represented masculine behavior in a female body in these scenes, while the rest of her performance was decidedly feminine. Likewise, her cockney Eliza had masculine elements, certainly in her feistiness with Freddy, and sparring with her father and Higgins, though she was thoroughly femme in her reshaped guise and sophisticated assertiveness. Where Mrs. Higgins remains the idealized mother, with wit but no song, Eliza becomes a flesh-and-blood woman – but one who is *made* and not *born* as such (Wolf 2002: 157). And her poignant appeal to Higgins for warm sensitivity and kindness can be read (as Wolf reads it) as a performance of desire and feminine sexuality.

In contrast with Eliza, Higgins is mainly the inviolable male chauvinist. His songs are the most emphatic, pointed expressions in lyric form of the character's unshakable belief in the authority and majesty of the English language, and in his own role as a proselytizing monarch of rhetoric. His songs depict different aspects of his character, and are therefore layered in a manner that is both charismatic and arrogant, making him seem intriguingly "charming and dislikeable at the same time" (McHugh 2012: 134). As in all his numbers, he enunciates exquisitely and expands his thesis on the relationship between language and social/cultural rank in formally intricate verse that transcends the superficial virtuosity and playfulness of the average patter-song – the type found so abundantly in Gilbert and Sullivan, for example. Of course, allied to this is his masculine imperialism. He is as assured of his own unimpeachable rank as master-dialectician as he is resolved to be immunized against women and their romantic sentimentality, which he considers a contemptible weakness. His gender imperialism is crystallized in his first number, "Why Can't the English . . .?," where he stops and re-starts the melody, pausing for a little patter on the side, and launching into full-blown *Sprechtstimme*, all the while consolidating his arrogant, manipulative personality. In his next big number, "I'm an Ordinary Man," Higgins reasserts his personality with suave urbanity and ironic wit, combining angular accuracy with falsifications in a sweet, genteel tone. There is something highly amusing about this alpha-male's claim of being ordinary, average, serene, gentle, even-tempered, and good-natured. But there is also something ironic in his lines:

> I'm a quiet living man
> Who prefers to spend his evenings
> In the silence of his room;
> Who likes an atmosphere as restful
> As an undiscovered tomb.

> A pensive man am I
> Of philosophic joys;
> Who likes to meditate,
> Contemplate,
> Free from humanity's mad, inhuman noise.
>
> (Lerner 1956: 58–9)

True, he is professorial and, therefore, inclined to philosophical thought in a broad sense, but his phrase "an undiscovered tomb" signifies something that he doesn't appear to recognize: a death-in-life. It is one thing to be solitary and detached from the tumult of humanity, but it is quite another to be thoroughly unsociable and without a life of social intercourse. And running throughout this song is his sinister misogyny, which Harrison was able to turn into something magisterial rather than disgusting.

This number describes the nefarious effects a woman would have upon him. The song is a brilliant set-piece of dramatically shifting registers and tones that require an actor-singer of mercurially quick tempi and modulations. Higgins claims to be "an ordinary man" of "no eccentric whim," who is "free of strife" until a woman interferes with his serenity. These phrases, with their gently measured amiability (ironic in terms of his true personality), amuse by their exaggeration. The self-idealization is warped. Then Higgins drops his placid composure to sound notes of turbulent gender conflicts and abrupt rage. Here the *allegro molto vivo* establishes his misogyny by periodic phrasing and brassy orchestration. A transitional pattern is repeated so that the passages of sweetness alternate with those of stormy irascibility, until, with the cresting passion and tempo, Higgins becomes increasingly onomatopoeic, rapidly piling up images of loud discord. He develops a mimetic pitch (in Rex Harrison's performance) on "She'll have a large Wagnerian mother / With a voice that shatters glass!" so that his voice takes on a shattering quality, and then he turns on all the laboratory machines at full volume, resulting in a cacophony. The song ends with a single statement of unflinching bravado: "I shall never let a woman in my life!" (Lerner 1956: 56–9).

Yet Higgins is the one who comes closest to a romantic ballad, and it is his songs that begin to interpret the Pygmalion myth. His song-soliloquy ("I've Grown Accustomed to Her Face") begins in terror as he curses himself for having a feeling that he had previously shut out of his soul: "Damn! Damn! Damn! Damn! / I've grown accustomed to her face!" (Lerner 1956: 181). Higgins finds himself startled by his own spontaneous feeling, but what a strange way of naming his ardor! His word "accustomed" suggests that his relationship with Eliza has more to do with mundane habit or repetition than with real ecstasy. Of course, there is unquestionably a layer of bemusement in a man who has disciplined himself to react more to words than to feelings. There is also, possibly, a buddy subtext at work, for Higgins has been so used to his own company or to having Pickering in a celibate *ménage-à-deux* (homo-sociality) that he has no experience in dealing with romantic heterosexuality. Whenever he has a problem with Eliza, he seeks his mother's counsel or moral support, though she invariably puts him in his place and takes Eliza's side.

His misogyny can be called into question when he shows the first sign of recognizing Eliza as a human, and thereby "catches the first glimpse of common humanity" in himself when he acknowledges that she is tired, that her head aches, that her nerves are "as raw as meat in a butcher's window" (Lerner 1956: 86); but he continues with his drill until

Eliza quite unexpectedly gets the drill correct, resulting in glorious relief for her, Higgins, and Pickering with "The Rain in Spain," which (as Swain says) "caps the joy of creation" (Swain 1990: 186). There is a subtle gesture just prior to the Embassy Ball when Eliza, decked out in a stunning gown and accoutrements, appears at the top of the stairs. Pickering declares that she looks beautiful, and then prompts Higgins for his agreement: "Don't you think so, Higgins?" But the Pygmalion, with characteristic reserve, musters a "Not bad. Not bad at all." This is a slight sign of a change in Higgins's attitude to Eliza, but it remains within his perspective or point of view as the master of phonetics and scientific experiment. Higgins appears to be assessing Eliza as the object of his unfinished experiment. The crucial gesture is then delivered through business described in the stage directions: "Higgins goes to the desk for his carnation which he slips into his button-hole, then looking furtively around to make certain Pickering doesn't see him, he pours himself a quick glass of port. He starts briskly for the door. At the threshold, he pauses, turns and gazes at Eliza. He returns to her and offers his arm. She takes it and they go out the door, Pickering following after" (Lerner 1956: 118). The stage directions indicate a more appealing human side to Higgins, shown by his furtive business with the port – coming after he had recently turned down Pickering's offer of the drink – and his silent but palpable acknowledgment of a transformed Eliza. He finally begins to treat her like a lady, extending her gracious courtesy that is virtually courtly. She is no longer merely an experiment but a flesh-and-blood woman – one he is now prepared to accompany to a fancy social event. However, this does not imply an intrinsic or unequivocal romantic connection.

The "creation" of a new woman ends with Eliza's solo release, "I Could Have Danced All Night," which not only expresses her joy in her own achievement, but also becomes the "first hint of Eliza's almost paradoxical attraction to Higgins" (Swain 1990: 189). This number prepares an audience to expect a more serious second act, at least as far as any dramatic resolution is concerned regarding her relationship with Higgins. Lerner and Loewe's libretto reprises Eliza's escapist fantasy in "Just You Wait" and "Wouldn't It Be Loverly?" in the second act in order to highlight her torment and to show that, while she is deeply affected, Higgins appears to be relatively untouched – though, of course, this impression proves to be false, given his ultimate consideration of "her looks," "her voice," and "her face" in "I've Grown Accustomed to Her Face," where his soul is stirred enough to mark his new wonder at himself and at her effect on him. This solo turned out to be Harrison's favorite in the show because it provided him with a perfect way of showing

> the bewilderment of the average Englishman of Higgins's time and class when confronted with anything at all to do with the life of the emotions. Because there are traces of pain, or at least genuine feeling behind the bewilderment, the audience, especially the hard-boiled ones who have had their emotions similarly repressed, were often moved to tears.
>
> (Harrison 1991: 154)

In this number (a miniature comedy-drama in itself), Higgins imagines how Eliza's life would collapse without him. He imagines her married to Freddy and living in "a wretched little flat above a store" (Lerner 1956: 182). He dwells on the prospect of her reverting to a life of poverty, abandonment, and humiliation, his *Schadenfreude* crackling at the very idea. But his song-soliloquy is also an examination of conscience or, at least, of his own probable reaction should she ever return penitently to him in order to seek his compassion and forgiveness. The alternating currents of benevolence and vindictiveness make for a marvelously vibrant soliloquy, streaked with despair and yearning as he voices the core refrain: "I've grown accustomed to her face." Joseph Swain shows how the melody of this number is "a transformation of 'Just You Wait,'" thereby raising a crucial question whether this "turnabout on the revenge motive" implies "a mutual affinity between the two protagonists" or is merely the implication that "Higgins's emotional maturity is at a stage comparable to Eliza's at the beginning of the play" (Swain 1990: 196–7). In other words, the two have reversed roles – as Lerner himself realized. Higgins goes through as much of a transformation as Eliza but "in a far less tangible way" because Shaw "would never allow the transformation to run its natural cause [*sic*]" (Lerner 1956: n.p.).

As we have seen, Eliza has not been a mere block that her Pygmalion carves into something physically beautiful; she herself has, figuratively, become a sculptor who has worked magic on Higgins, turning him from a block of pedantic learning into a human being with a ruffled soul. Of course, as Stacy Wolf accurately notes, their relationship, while "intense and engaged . . . is purely utilitarian and entirely unerotic" (Wolf 2002: 155). It is always Eliza who wants romance while it is Higgins who wants success in his experiment. And when you add the figure of Pickering to the mix, it is easy to see why the only consummation or eroticism in the relationship, which is generally triangular, is the tango of "The Rain in Spain," for tango has always had a sexual connotation – though the manner in which Lerner and Loewe devised it, Moss Hart staged it, and the performers essayed it, this tango celebrated masculine dominance. As the stage directions show, Higgins is the matador while Pickering plays the bull. Eliza is used by the men to celebrate what they construe as their victorious experiment rather than her triumph. She is grabbed by Higgins to do "a few awkward tango steps," while Pickering "jumps around like a flamenco dancer." Then Eliza is swung onto a sofa only so that Higgins can join Pickering in "a bit of heel-clicking." It is only then that "a wild jig" breaks out by all three before they collapse in mirth upon the sofa (Lerner 1956: 88).

The ending of the musical returns to the question of romantic resolution without dispelling a sense of ambiguity. After Higgins has confronted his own palpable inner stirring about Eliza in "I've Grown Accustomed to Her Face," to a degree that alarms him and fills him with despair, he is shown in the final scene to be in his study where he listens to her voice recorded on one of his machines as he sits, hat still on, head bowed. It is precisely at this point that Eliza walks softly into the room and catches his recorded line: "It's almost irresistible. She's so deliciously low, so horribly dirty." Eliza turns off the machine, utters her line about having washed her face and hands before arriving, and takes note of Higgins's body language, though not necessarily of his inner emotions. The stage directions capture this dichotomy:

> Higgins straightens up. If he could but let himself, his face would radiate unmistakable relief and joy. If he could but let himself, he would run to her. Instead, he leans back with a contented sigh pushing his hat forward till it almost covers his face.

He then asks softly: "Eliza, where the devil are my slippers?" (Lerner 1958: 186). Lerner and Loewe have fashioned the sense of a conventional ending, but with no romantic duet, no physical touching, and no verbalizing about love. It works in context because it suggests that the two characters have an amity or cordial relationship at last. But much depends on the manner in which this ending is staged. Lerner writes in the stage directions that Eliza (with "tears in her eyes") "understands," though he neglects to spell out what she understands. In Lerner's view, Higgins really wanted a friend rather than a wife or lover because he didn't understand the emotional pressure of an intimate relationship. He was content to remain "serenely independent."

I wish to focus on the chinks that the prospect of this independence finds in Higgins's sturdy, masculine armor. Prior to the finale, he has indicated a weakness, a susceptibility to feeling hurt or pain. In the fifth scene of Act II, during the blazing row with Eliza, he continues to assert his male dominance by warning that if she chooses to return, he shall continue treating her the way he always has. If she leaves, he will miss her because he has learned something from her "idiotic notions" (Lerner 1956: 172–4). It is clear that Higgins runs the gamut of feeling from superiority, emotional sadism, blustering heartlessness, and stubborn intransigence to soft questioning and modest acknowledgment or humility (tempered immediately, nevertheless, by his unyielding masculine intelligence). Eliza remains "idiotic" even while she has taught him something crucial about himself. In subsequent passages in the same scene, he associates Eliza and other women with "snivelling" sentimentality.

For her part, Eliza does not crave marriage ("I wouldn't marry you if you asked me; and you're nearer his age than what [Freddy] is") but "a little kindness," pleasantness, and friendship (Lerner 1956: 175–6). When she articulates her craving, Higgins immediately identifies it with what he and Pickering feel: a benevolent homo-sociality, implying that she can share the same arrangement with them. But there's another eruption from Eliza, provoking Higgins's awe and wonder at her newfound audacity and inner strength: "Eliza, you're magnificent! Five minutes ago you were a millstone around my neck. Now you're a tower of strength, a consort battleship! I like you like this!" (Lerner 1956: 179). A strange romance, indeed, for Higgins's ardor is for things that are impersonal: tower and battleship, things that are metallic or hard and rigid. While admiring her hard qualities (Lerner describes her as staring "stonily" at Higgins), he continues to eschew her essential humanity. He calls on his mother to help him after Eliza's exit, before making the "terrifying discovery" in "I've Grown Accustomed to Her Face." So, ultimately, it is her "divine fire," and not his, that stirs his soul.

The ending of this musical places Eliza in an interesting position. Does her return to Higgins mean that she will continue to be subservient to him and at his beck and call, or does it mean that since he is now able to see her as a consort, her return is not exactly a capitulation or surrender to his alpha-male ego but, rather, a sly victory of her own? The question is whether she should behave at the end like an efficient owner of a flower shop or like one of the Ascot ladies. Should she be subservient in all essential details to Higgins, or should she be true to her feisty, feminist core, adopting only the social manner of the upper class, while privately enjoying a psychological equality with Higgins, with concomitant emotional superiority?

When the curtain descends as Eliza's eyes fill with tears, she is supposed to "understand" her and Higgins's accommodation with reality. But why do her eyes fill with tears? Is she grateful to have Higgins's companionship? Or is she tacitly willing to find her place in the triangulation with Pickering at Wimpole Street? The very fact that she is on the verge of tears indicates feeling, and there is a veiled suggestion that it is love behind that feeling. Higgins's final song-soliloquy ("I've Grown Accustomed to Her Face") already dramatized this point. However, the conclusion is far less a romantic closure than Lerner and Loewe intended it to be.

What tone should Eliza use in what many an audience may read as her submission or compliance? While it is Higgins who replays their early conversation about her need for elocution lessons – a gesture of woeful nostalgia – it is Eliza who turns off the machine upon her entrance in the final scene, and she repeats a line she had once used early in the story: "I washed my face and hands before I come, I did" (Lerner 1956: 186). Now her tone is not a protest but a gentle reminder of a time past when he had utter control and dominion over her until she learned to find out some of his character flaws as a man and how to speak for herself as one whose life is at stake. Higgins thinks he has created or put together a person who will slavishly follow his dictates, but he discovers that what he has helped create is not a thing or commodity but a human being, a woman with a soul who helps him find his – at least for a time. There is never any question of sexual congress between the two, and without sex, *My Fair Lady* remains a romance more as unrequited longing than as actual fact, despite its chandeliers and "The Embassy Waltz."

Conclusion

My Fair Lady evidently brought into focus areas that were important for Andrews, Harrison, and Hart: self-doubt, romance (in various connotations), creativity, and artistic success. The fact that the Broadway original left an indelible sense of romance was due, in large part, to the performances of Andrews and Harrison, and the subtle direction of Moss Hart. Both stars were unequivocally English throughout the show, with Andrews growing stronger in the role, as encouraged by the libretto and her eventual self-confidence. Her singing voice made her a match for Harrison's bravura speaking voice, though she could never match his comic timing or shadings of characterization. Where many thought she was the best Eliza in a *My Fair Lady* production, she confessed that she couldn't remember a single performance when she didn't wonder if she could get through it or if by saving her voice in a small song she would have enough voice left for a big one. Despite her doubts, she triumphed, but never again — not in *Camelot* (where she was directed in 1960 by Hart once again in yet another libretto by Lerner) or in *Victor/Victoria* (where, opening on Broadway in 1995, she would offer a flamboyant transvestite turn) – would she ever enjoy such an overwhelming success. Andrews had never played a major role in an American musical, and she was filled with grave self-doubts early in rehearsals until Moss Hart assumed the role of directorial Pygmalion to her Galatea. However, she was determined, worked hard, exuded charm, and once she scrubbed out the grime and was dressed in tiara and resplendent gown for the Embassy Ball, she became an overnight sensation. She looked beautifully nubile, though her role denied her the traditional lyrics for romantic love, and even though the ending of the musical suggested a romantic liaison between her and Harrison's Higgins, she remained virginal on stage, her passion reserved more for her rages against Higgins than for any declaration of love. She was feisty, ardent, and sweet – an angel of song who spread her wings to rapturous ovations. In terms of sexual suggestiveness, she was always femme, but the musical denied her the consolation of a real heterosexual union with her counterpart.

In the show, she was a common girl learning to be a sophisticated woman, and she was also learning to teach a man to be a real man and not simply a mouthpiece for ideas and biases. But all her virtues as a performer at that time had cultural associations with virginity and whiteness. If Eliza could not be a malleable doll for Higgins, she could, perhaps, have been the angel of the house. And Andrews certainly projected an almost angelic purity of personality and voice. Earlier in her career, in the television *Cinderella*, she was persuasively feminine in a manner that Stacy Wolf characterizes as a "queering" of a western narrative: a narrative that "rewards martyrdom and passivity, portrays love as instantaneous and perfect, and values heterosexual marriage above all" (Wolf 2002: 141). In *Camelot*, she portrayed Guenevere "in a half-serious, half-mocking way," contradicting by her own sweet soprano Guenevere's passionate desire for sex and delight that causes men to fight violently over her (Wolf 2002: 167). Even off-stage, she maintained a squeaky-clean image, resisting Robert Goulet (her Lancelot), who had a crush on her, and Richard Burton (whose advice she sought on the matter, even though Burton himself tried unsuccessfully to woo and seduce her) (Stirling 2007: 109).

She would later capitalize on her goody-goody, non-sexual image as the very English Mary Poppins who flies over London with a bottomless carpet-bag and an umbrella in the 1964 film, and as an exuberantly youthful Maria in the movie version of *The Sound of Music* (1965). In the latter case, she once again failed to look erotic opposite her male co-star – Christopher Plummer – who (before his much later change of heart) remarked with a distinct lack of chivalry: "Working with her was like getting hit over the head with a Hallmark card" (Stirling 2007: 144). James Garner, her leading man in her second film, *The Americanization of Emily* (1964; actu-ally filmed between *Mary Poppins* and *The Sound of Music*), also could not muster enough sexual chemistry with her to liberate her from her prissy white image, even though she was playing a woman who slept around a lot and behaved like a tramp. Pauline Kael said acidly of her Emily: "Julie Andrews could play a promiscuous girl and shine with virtue" (Stirling 2007: 149).

She also failed to strike romantic sparks opposite Paul Newman in Hitchcock's *Torn Curtain* (1966), an undistin-guished spy film, provoking a critic to mock that her scene in bed with Newman was "as shocking as seeing Shirley Temple kicking the cat" (Stirling 2007: 191). Although her close friends attested to her bawdy wit in private, she could not seem to overcome her image of chaste virtue. Gossip columnist Joyce Haber made a notorious effort to "dirty" up Andrews's image, spreading rumours about Andrews and Edwards's sexual preferences, suggesting that Andrews, her second husband Blake Edwards, and Rock Hudson were a sexual threesome, and, further, that Edwards and Hudson had been gay lovers in San Francisco. (Blake Edwards did admit in the Christmas 1982 issue of *Playboy* that he had had "some homosexual fantasies" in his younger days [Stirling 2007: 277]). Though livid, Andrews retorted with crisp British wit: "They should give Haber open-heart surgery, and go in through the feet" (Stirling 2007: 219).

But Andrews's sang-froid outweighed her sexiness on screen. The closest she would come to eroticism was in *Victor/Victoria* (both on film in 1982 and on Broadway in 1995), directed by Edwards, who had once dismissed her as "so sweet, she probably has violets between her legs" (White 1998: 109). Playing a singer who has fallen on hard times and who must pretend to be a man pretending to be a woman in order to survive, she was thoroughly credible as the woman and surprisingly bold in her masculine impersonation. Her transvestite performance was alluring, especially in the opening number, "Le Jazz Hot," set inside a 1930s Parisian nightclub. This was an irony, to be sure, for in a woman's skin and in a female role, she could not be sexually arousing, but in a man's trousers, she could at least stir up double meanings queerly. If, as Eliza, it took a man to compel her to discover her inner fire, it was only while dressed as a man that Andrews could project sexuality, however ambiguously and disturbingly to her most ardent fans.

Harrison, of course, was a past master of high comedy, and though he had his own insecurities as far as singing was concerned, he cleverly disguised these when on stage by his peculiar mode of spoken song. Higgins became his signature role. However, as a man he remained difficult: vituperative, domineering, irascible, and self-centered. Kenneth Tynan once recorded in his diaries a joke conceived "in the loo" about a possible *Variety* headline if Harrison were to slug an autograph collector: "SHIT HITS FAN" (Tynan 2001: 26). The sentimental was not part of Harrison's natural repertoire, and even on his deathbed he remained uncompromisingly nasty, barking out a "Drop Dead!" to his older son Carey, who had made the error of asking if there was anything he could do for his father. Consistent with himself, he then gestured to his younger son Noel to approach his bed, and murmured: "And by the way, Noel, there was something I always wanted to tell you. I could never stand the sound of your fucking guitar" (Garland 1998: 215). To Carey, his father's star qualities were rooted in a "thin, sad soul of a shallow humanity" (Garland 1998: 217). In other words, there was an essential loneliness in his father, and this is what Harrison revealed at times as Higgins, the epitome of rampant egocentricity, for whom Plato, tuning forks, recording machines, and books count for more than other humans.

Given his reputation as "sexy Rexy," an audience could presume romance between him and Julie Andrews's Eliza, even though the libretto gives no express indication of this, apart from the business of his offering her his arm as they leave for the Embassy Ball, and the suggestion of a settled domestic arrangement at the end when she returns to him. Forced to play a confirmed bachelor and to confide in Pickering rather than in Eliza, the actor was nevertheless able to make Higgins seem seductively sexual by his expert modulations of tone and rhythm, his assertiveness with a cowering Eliza, his awakened sense of her dignity and disarming candor, and his eventual acknowledgment that she has come to mean more to him than he had ever dreamed was possible. But Harrison remained in control of his scenes, whether with Eliza or anyone else, allowing nobody to poach his theatrical territory, except for Holloway's Doolittle, because there was simply no way to steal a scene from that rogue, who had his own lowlife seductive power.

Patrick Garland identified "a close connection between the art of high comedy and a capacity for rage," and noted that rage always played a dominant part in Harrison's romantic relationships (Garland 1998: 237) – as does Higgins's anger in his relationship with Eliza. An audience was not altogether certain that this Higgins would not attempt to smash Eliza if she did not do his bidding. Offstage, most of the time events and people went the way he wanted them to – especially in his philandering – and God help those on stage who got in his way, which is to say in his spotlight. Though his life was sometimes marked by disappointment, dismay, and tragedy – as in the suicides of lover Carol Landis and his fourth wife, Rachel Roberts, and the premature death of Kay Kendall, possibly his most beloved wife – Harrison remained the unrepentant alpha male – the sexy heterosexual with scarcely an apology to anyone. How uncharacteristic, then, for him to have played a confirmed bachelor who never gets to make love to the heroine! Yet many who saw his bravura performance in *My Fair Lady* were convinced that Higgins was in love with Eliza. But, perhaps, what was really behind their imaginings was what Kenneth Tynan caught in the film version: "that combination of the aggressor and the injured, the schoolmaster and the truant, which adds up in Britain (and elsewhere) to erotic infallibility" (Tynan 1967: 213).

Where Harrison remained the alpha male on stage and off, Moss Hart remained discreet, his directorial hand "everywhere present and everywhere unobtrusive" (Bach 2001: 364). Based on their collaboration on two famous Broadway musicals, Alan J. Lerner described Hart's directorial authority in rehearsals as being

> total, not because he demanded it but because it was so apparent to everyone he knew what he was doing. If an actor suggested a better move, Moss was the first one to recognize it and be grateful. He was the only director I ever knew who could walk up on the stage and say to the actors: "I haven't a clue what to do with this scene. Does anyone have an idea?" – and not lose his authority. (Brown 2006: 347)

In private rehearsals with Andrews, who was floundering in her role, he was never shy to illustrate exactly what he wanted from her. He would stomp up on stage to interrupt her futile attempts at acting, and show her exactly how to growl "Aaaooowww," hit out at an imaginary Higgins, and hold a teacup primly and properly, with the little finger extended. He also knew how to pacify an increasingly maddened and neurotic Harrison, who clearly felt that his Eliza was nowhere near her part and was not fit to share the stage with him. When Harrison screamed at him in front of other members of the company, Hart did not flinch. Instead, he quietly warned the actor: "I'm a writer. If we're going to get into this territory, I can do it a good deal better and more cruelly than you can." As he wrote later, he was content to be "the custodian of the proceedings on stage, not the star of them" (Bach 2001: 364), but the show had such deep relevance to his own life that his success as director cannot be diminished. Hart was no less sexually ambiguous than the romance unfolding in the musical, and though there was no physical liaison with Julie Andrews, he served as her Pygmalion, bringing her performance to life, giving her the confidence to seem assured in her singing and acting opposite Harrison, the alpha male. Hart also had to deal with Stanley Holloway, who continued to feel aggrieved at being "neglected."

Hart was superb at capitalizing on the cast's body language: "Scenes involving the proletariat looked and moved differently from those for the gentry: the 'knees up' abandon of the chorus work in 'A Little Bit of Luck' compared dissonantly with the rigid comportment of the Ascot folk" (Mordden 2013: 196). He was also responsible for much of the polishing done on the libretto, often by way of cutting songs that did not work well in the show or weakened the structure. Although Lerner gets credit for the stage directions in the published libretto, it is probably Moss Hart who should be receiving the lion's share for his directorial contribution. Years later, Hart's production manager, Stone ("Bud") Widney, described Hart's ability to maintain objectivity and focus by working as if he had two heads: one for the details, and the other for "pulling back and just view[ing] [the show] like an audience does" (Brown 2006: 356). Perhaps his greatest directorial coup was with "The Rain in Spain" number because its comedy and drama were so infectious that audiences could never resist cheering, laughing, screaming, whooping, and applauding so vociferously as to literally stop the show. His mixture of the light and subtle became the "high-water mark of taste in the Broadway theater" (Bach 2001: 363).

In terms of his own creativity, Hart discovered a new brio because during the Philadelphia tryout, he worked with growing confidence on his autobiography (*Act One*), which Random House was awaiting eagerly. Despite his anxieties about declining health, *My Fair Lady* had put him back on top of Broadway, and he continued to rehearse his incantation about how he had gone from hardship and struggle in the Bronx to a life of material and artistic success – a life that had becalmed the stresses of his sexual ambiguity, and one that continued to allow him the flamboyance of a mink-lined raincoat, movie-star panache, and an unabashed joy in his existential journey. All this while he continued to indulge in mischief with sexual overtones when directing *Camelot*, urging Roddy McDowall to repeatedly walk across the stage and exit merely so that Hart could watch him "twinkle" his ass (Bach 2001: 376). This direction did nothing to assist McDowall with characterization, but it confirmed Hart's charming flirtatiousness and active sexual interest – something he could not indulge with macho Harrison.

His passion was for theatre, and though he had an active sex life offstage (more homoerotic than heterosexual), he let romance simmer in the background of the musical. In a sense he was as asexual as Higgins. He certainly delayed committing himself to marriage, tying the knot when he was already middle-aged. His wooing of and marriage to Kitty Carlisle had a distinctly unromantic and non-dramatic tone. In an interview, Carlisle divulged (in an unguarded moment) that neither she nor Hart had been in love with each other when they married in 1946. The whole business of their marriage was pragmatic: the right thing to do at that time, leaving it to time for love to follow (Bach 2001: 268). Hart was never as candid about the matter. His biographer asserts that Hart habitually treated her as "a decorative accessory to a life no less self-indulgent than bachelorhood had been, though it was a role she eagerly accepted" (Bach 2001: 271). The intersection of biography and *My Fair Lady* could hardly be clearer, especially as Higgins regards Eliza as a decorative trophy by which to win his bet with Pickering, while he indulges the habits of bachelorhood. Just as Higgins eventually moves from rampaging egotism to a more relaxed complacency when Eliza returns to him, so Moss Hart moved away from the "mischievous iconoclasm of his youth" to a relatively comfortable middle age, though his public image still dazzled. At Rex Harrison's final performance in the original Broadway run, Harrison's bride of six months, Kay Kendall, went on stage unannounced as the queen of Transylvania in the Embassy Ball scene. Her escort – also unannounced – was Hart. It was his final appearance on a Broadway stage. As with Andrews, he failed to repeat the phenomenal success of *My Fair Lady*, for his swan song, *Camelot*, was hardly in the same league. Nor did he have time for a bigger hit; he collapsed from a coronary at age 57.

My Fair Lady confirmed that love and work were synonymous for Moss Hart, and that the theatre offered (in the words of his biographer) "refuge from an otherwise inhospitable world" (Bach 2001: 386). Like Julie Andrews, he had two "fathers": his biological one, Barnett Hart, and his mentor-collaborator, George S. Kaufman. He and Andrews were also to share another link years later: like him, she needed recourse to psychoanalysis – though in her case, this transpired in the 1960s, after Hart's death, and was not widely known, as she struggled to find out why she was not happy with her enormous success (White 1998: 111). Like Andrews, he discovered that theatre could lead to a glittering, transforming world, though in his case, that world was far wider and more splendidly personified in his own life. He did things to get them right because that was what he knew how to do and what he loved doing. But unlike Harrison, he never needed to be a demon to achieve this. The only demons he possessed were sexual or neurotic anxieties that affected him rather than being passed on to other possible victims. He paid dearly at the end with his physical and mental health, but he remained a dazzler to his dying day.

References

Alpert, Hollis, 1991. *Broadway! 125 Years of Musical Theatre.* New York: Little, Brown.

Andrews, Julie, 2008. *Home: A Memoir of My Early Years.* New York: Hyperion.

Anon, 1956a. Review of *My Fair Lady. Variety*, March 21.

Anon, 1956b. "Moon over Wimpole Street." Review of *My Fair Lady, Saturday Review*, April 7.

Atkinson, Brooks, 1956a. "Everybody's 'Lady.'" *New York Times*, June 3.

Atkinson, Brooks, 1956b. "My Fair Lady." *New York Times*, March 16.

Bach, Steven, 2001. *Dazzler: The Life and Times of Moss Hart.* New York: Alfred A. Knopf.

Beaton, Cecil, 1964. *Cecil Beaton's "Fair Lady."* London: Weidenfeld.

Beaton, Cecil, 1976. *The Restless Years: Diaries 1955–63.* London: Weidenfeld.

Beaton, Cecil, 1989. *The Glass of Fashion.* London: Cassell.

Beaton, Cecil, 2003. *Beaton in the Sixties: More Unexpurgated Diaries.* London: Weidenfeld and Nicolson.

Beaufort, John, 1956. "*My Fair Lady* from *Pygmalion*." *Christian Science Monitor*, March 24.

Beckerman, Bernard, and Howard Siegman, eds., 1983. *On Stage: Selected Theatre Reviews from the New York Times 1920–1970.* New York: Arno.

Bentley, Eric, 1957. *Bernard Shaw.* New York: New Directions.

Bentley, Eric, 1958. "My Fair Lady." *Modern Drama* 1.2: 135–36.

Bentley, Eric, 1984. *What Is Theatre?* New York: Limelight.

Block, Geoffrey, 1997. *Enchanted Evenings: The Broadway Musical from "Show Boat" to Sondheim*. New York: Oxford University Press.

Bordman, Gerald, 1978. *American Musical Theatre*. New York: Oxford University Press.

Brahms, Caryl, 1958. "Fair Lady-Mindedness." *Plays and Players* 5.9: 7.

Brockes, Emma, 2007. *What Would Barbra Do?: How Musicals Changed My Life*. New York: HarperCollins.

Brown, Jared, 2006. *Moss Hart: A Prince of the Theatre*. New York: Back Stage Books.

Buckle, Richard, ed., 1982. *Self-Portrait with Friends: Selected Diaries of Cecil Beaton 1926–1974*. Harmondsworth: Penguin.

Burton, Richard, 2012. *The Richard Burton Diaries*. Ed. Chris Williams. New Haven and London: Yale University Press.

Castle, Charles, 1972. *Noel*. London: W. H. Allen.

Chapman, John, 1956. "*My Fair Lady* a Superb, Stylish Musical Play with a Perfect Cast." *Daily News* [New York], March 16.

Chesterton, G. K., 1958. *George Bernard Shaw*. New York: Hill and Wang.

Clum, John M., 1999. *Something for the Boys: Musical Theater and Gay Culture*. New York: St. Martin's.

Coleman, Robert, 1956. "*My Fair Lady* Is a Glittering Musical." *Daily Mirror*, March 16.

Dash, Thomas R., 1956. Review of *My Fair Lady*. *Women's Wear Daily*, March 16.

Eliot, Marc, 2004. *Cary Grant: A Biography*. New York: Harmony Books.

Engel, Lehman, 1972. *Words with Music*. New York: Macmillan.

Ewen, David, 1959. *Complete Book of the American Musical Theatre*. Rev. edn. New York: Holt.

Feuer, Cy with Ken Gross, 2003. *I Got the Show Right Here*. New York: Applause.

Ganzl, Kurt, 1990. *The Blackwell Guide to the Musical Theatre on Record*. Oxford: Blackwell.

Garber, Marjorie, 2005. *Shakespeare after All*. New York: Anchor Books.

Garebian, Keith, 1992. *The Making of "My Fair Lady."* Toronto: ECW Press.

Garland, Patrick, 1998. *The Incomparable Rex: A Memoir of Rex Harrison in the 1980s*. London: Macmillan.

Garner, James and Jon Winokur, 2011. *The Garner Files: A Memoir*. New York: Simon and Schuster.

Gibbs, Wolcott, 1956. "Shaw with Music." *New Yorker*, March 24.

Gielgud, John, 2004. *Gielgud's Letters*. Ed. and intro. Richard Mangan. London: Weidenfeld and Nicolson.

Gottfried, Martin, 1979. *Broadway Musicals*. New York: Abrams.

Green, Benny, ed., 1987. *A Hymn to Him: The Lyrics of Alan Jay Lerner*. London: Pavilion.

Green, Stanley, 1974. *The World of Musical Comedy*. 3rd rev. edn. New York: Barnes.

Green, Stanley, 1976. *Encyclopedia of the Musical Theatre*. New York: Da Capo, 1976.

Guernsey, Otis L., Jr., 1987. *Curtain Times: The New York Theatre 1965–1987*. New York: Applause.

Hadleigh, Boze, 1986. *Conversations with My Elders*. New York: St. Martin's.

Harrison, Rex, 1975. *Rex: An Autobiography*. London: Macmillan.

Harrison, Rex, 1991. *A Damned Serious Business*. New York: Bantam.

Hart, Kitty Carlisle, 1988. *Kitty: An Autobiography*. New York: Doubleday.

Hart, Moss, 1959. *Act One: An Autobiography*. New York: Random House.

Hart, Moss and Ira Gershwin, 1941. *Lady in the Dark*. New York: Random House.

Hawkins, William, 1956. "*My Fair Lady* Is a Smash Hit." *New York World Telegram and the Sun*, March 16.

Hirschhorn, Clive, 1991. *The Hollywood Musical* (revised and updated). New York: Portland House.

Hischak, Thomas, 2008. *The Oxford Companion to the American Musical: Theatre, Film, and Television*. New York: Oxford University Press.

Holloway, Stanley, 1967. *Wiv a Little Bit o' Luck*. London: Leslie Frewin.

Holroyd, Michael, 1979. *The Genius of Shaw*. London: Hodder.

Holroyd, Michael, 1989. *The Pursuit of Power: 1898–1918*. Vol. II of *Bernard Shaw*. London: Chatto.

Holroyd, Michael, 1992. *The Last Laugh: 1950–1991*. Vol. IV of *Bernard Shaw*. London: Chatto.

Holroyd, Michael, 1991. *The Lure of Fantasy: 1918–1950*. Vol. II of *Bernard Shaw*. London: Chatto.

Irvine, William, 1949. *The Universe of G. B. S.* New York: Whittlesey.

Jackson, Arthur, 1977. *The Best Musicals: From "Show Boat" to "A Chorus Line."* New York: Crown.

Kaufman, R. J., ed., 1965. *G. B. Shaw: A Collection of Critical Essays.* Englewood Cliffs, NJ: Prentice.

Kennedy, Matthew, 2014. *Road-Show: The Fall of Film Musicals in the 1960s.* New York: Oxford University Press.

Kerr, Walter, 1956. "*My Fair Lady.*" *Herald Tribune* [New York], March 16.

Kerr, Walter, 1979. *Journey to the Center of the Theatre.* New York: Knopf.

Knapp, Raymond, 2005. *The American Musical and the Formation of National Identity.* Princeton, NJ: Princeton University Press, 2005.

Knapp, Raymond, 2006. *The American Musical and the Performance of Personal Identity.* Princeton, NJ: Princeton University Press.

Kronenberger, Louis, 1952. *The Thread of Laughter: Chapters on English Stage Comedy from Jonson to Maugham.* New York: Knopf.

Laufe, Abe, 1970. *Broadway's Greatest Musicals.* New York: Funk.

Leary, Daniel, ed., 1983. *Shaw's Plays in Performance.* Vol. III of *Annual of Bernard Shaw Studies.* University Park, PA: Pennsylvania State University Press.

Lees, Gene, 1990. *Inventing Champagne: The Worlds of Lerner and Loewe.* New York: St. Martin's.

Lerner, Alan Jay, 1956. "Shavian Musical Notes," *New York Times*, March 11.

Lerner, Alan Jay, 1957. "Programme Note." *Playbill* 1.6: 17.

Lerner, Alan Jay, 1958. *My Fair Lady: A Musical Play in Two Acts.* New York: Coward–McCann.

Lerner, Alan Jay, 1978. *The Street where I Live.* London: Hodder.

Lerner, Alan Jay, 1986. *The Musical Theatre: A Celebration.* New York: McGraw.

Mast, Gerald, 1987. *Can't Help Singin': The American Musical on Stage and Screen.* Woodstock: Overlook.

McCarthy, Desmond, 1951. *Shaw.* London: MacGibbon and Kee.

McClain, John, 1956. "It's Fetching – Well Done!" *New York Journal-American*, March 16.

McClung, Bruce D., 2007. *Lady in the Dark: Biography of a Musical.* New York: Oxford University Press.

McHugh, Dominic, 2012. *Loverly: The Life and Times of "My Fair Lady."* New York: Oxford University Press.

Meisel, Martin, 1984. *Shaw and the Nineteenth Century Theatre*. New York: Limelight.

Mordden, Ethan, 1981. *The Hollywood Musical*. New York: St. Martin's.

Mordden, Ethan, 1983. *Broadway Babies: The People who Made the American Musical*. New York: Oxford University Press.

Mordden, Ethan, 2013. *Anything Goes: A History of American Musical Theatre*. New York: Oxford University Press.

Morgan, Margery M., 1972. *The Shavian Playground: An Exploration of the Art of George Bernard Shaw*. London: Methuen.

Morley, Sheridan, 1974 [1969]. *A Talent to Amuse: A Biography of Noel Coward*. Harmondsworth: Penguin.

Mugglestone, Lynda, 1993. "Shaw, Subjective Inequality, and the Social Meanings of Language in *Pygmalion*." *Review of English Studies* 44.175: 373–83.

Nathan, George Jean, 1956a. "The Season's Top Show." *New York Journal-American*, March 31.

Nathan, George Jean, 1956b. Column in *New York Journal-American*, May 5.

Ovid, 1998 [1700]. *Metamorphoses*. Trans. John Dryden. London: Wordsworth Classics.

Paglia, Camille, 1991. *Sexual Personae: Art and Decadence from Nefertiti to Emily Dickinson*. New York: Vintage Books.

Pascal, Valerie, 1970. *The Disciple and His Devil*. New York: McGraw.

Pearson, Hesketh, 1942. *Bernard Shaw: His Life and Personality*. London: Collins.

S., F., 1958. Review of *My Fair Lady*. *Theatre World* 54.401: 23.

Secrest, Meryle, 2001. *Somewhere for Me: A Biography of Richard Rodgers*. New York: Applause.

Shaw, Bernard, 1962. *Complete Plays with Prefaces, Vol. I*. New York: Dodd, Mead.

Shaw, Bernard, 1963 [1900]. *Pygmalion*. Harmondsworth: Penguin.

Smith, Oliver, [1970]. "The Designer Talks." Interview with Robert Waterhouse. *Plays and Players* 18.2: 20–1.

Sondheim, Stephen, 2010. *Finishing the Hat: Collected Lyrics (1954–1981) with Attendant Comments, Principles, Heresies, Grudges, Whines and Anecdotes*. New York: Alfred A. Knopf.

Sorrell, Walter, 1969. *Hanya Holm: The Biography of an Artist*. Middletown, CT: Wesleyan University Press.

Stephens, Frances, ed., 1958. *Theatre World Annual*. Vol. IX. London: Rockcliff.

Steyn, Mark, 2000. *Broadway Babies Say Goodnight: Musicals Then and Now*. London: Faber and Faber.

Stirling, Richard, 2007. *Julie Andrews: An Intimate Biography*. London: Portrait.

Suskin, Steven, 1990. *Opening Night on Broadway*. New York: Schirmer.

Swain, Joseph P., 1990. *The Broadway Musical: A Critical and Musical Survey*. New York: Oxford University Press.

Tynan, Kenneth, 1967. *Tynan Right and Left*. London: Longmans.

Tynan, Kenneth, 1976. *A View of the English Stage*. Frogmore: Paladin.

Tynan, Kenneth, 2001. *The Diaries of Kenneth Tynan*. Ed. John Lahr. London: Bloomsbury.

Valency, Maurice, 1983. *The Cart and the Trumpet: The Plays of George Bernard Shaw*. New York: Schocken.

Vickers, Hugo, 1985. *Cecil Beaton: The Authorized Biography*. London: Weidenfeld.

Watts, Richard, Jr., 1956. "When Everything Goes Right." *New York Post*, March 16.

Weintraub, Stanley, 1969. *Shaw: An Autobiography 1856–1898*. Vol. I. New York: Weybright and Talley.

Weintraub, Stanley, 1970. *The Playwright Years 1898–1950*. Vol. II. Or *Shaw: An Autobiography*. New York: Weybright and Talley.

White, Timothy, 1998. *The Entertainers: Portraits of Stardom in the 20th Century*. New York: Billboard Books.

Windeler, Robert, 1983. *Julie Andrews: A Biography*. New York: St. Martin's.

Wolf, Matt, 2001. Review of *My Fair Lady*. *Variety*, March 20.

Wolf, Stacy, 2002. *A Problem like Maria: Gender and Sexuality in the American Musical*. Ann Arbor, MI: University of Michigan Press.

Wolf, Stacy, 2011. *Changed for Good: A Feminist History of the Broadway Musical*. New York: Oxford University Press.

Zadan, Craig, 1989. *Sondheim & Co*. 2nd edn. New York: Harper.

Index